DATE DUE

MAR 20 74			
JUL 31 74			
JUN 9 76			
NOV 22 78			

Profile
of
F. Scott Fitzgerald

Compiled by

Matthew J. Bruccoli
University of South Carolina

Charles E. Merrill Publishing Company
A Bell & Howell Company
Columbus, Ohio

CHARLES E. MERRILL PROFILES

Under the General Editorship of
Matthew J. Bruccoli and Joseph Katz

The cover portrait by Gordon Bryant is from the collection of Matthew J. Bruccoli.

ISBN: 0-675-09263-9

Library of Congress Catalog Card Number: 75-139588

1 2 3 4 5 6 7 8 9—79 78 77 76 75 74 73 72 71

Printed in the United States of America

Preface

This collection provides material for study of two aspects of F. Scott Fitzgerald's career: (1) Fitzgerald as a man of letters: his intentions as an artist; (2) The reception and reputation of Fitzgerald's work: his critical image.

Such a collection is useful because Fitzgerald's career is cloaked in scandal and legend. That much of the gossip is true only obscures or distorts the student's view of the pro who in twenty years wrote five novels, two of them masterpieces, and 160-odd stories—the genius who sold off pieces of his talent while somehow preserving the best part; the artist who knew what he was doing.

The only relevant thing about F. Scott Fitzgerald is that he was "one of the greatest writers that ever lived." And writers matter more than other people.

My thanks are due to Jennifer Atkinson, Barbara Pinkwas, and I. S. Skelton.

M. J. B.

Contents

Re-read a lot of Scott Fitzgerald's work this week. God, I love that man. Damn fool critics are forever calling writers geniuses for their idiosyncracies—Hemingway for his reticent dialogue, Wolfe for his gargantuan energy, and so on. Fitzgerald's only idiosyncrasy was his pure brilliance.

—J. D. Salinger

Reprinted from a letter to Mrs. Elizabeth Murray, *Seventy* (New York: House of El Dieff, 1970), item # 78.

Chronicle of Events

1896   Born September 24, St. Paul, Minnesota.

1898-1908   Buffalo—Syracuse—Buffalo, New York.

1908-11   St. Paul Academy. First publication.

1911-13   Newman School, Hackensack, New Jersey.

1913-17   Princeton University. Wrote for *Princeton Tiger* and *Nassau Literary Magazine*; 3 Triangle Club shows. Met Edmund Wilson and John Peale Bishop. Did not receive degree.

1917-18   Army. Wrote first draft of novel. Met Zelda Sayre (born 1900) in the summer of 1918 when stationed at Camp Sheridan, near Montgomery, Alabama.

1919   Worked for New York ad agency; unable to marry because of finances; wrote stories. Quit job in July 1919 and returned to St. Paul to rewrite novel. *This Side of Paradise* accepted by Scribners in September. Sold stories.

1920   *This Side of Paradise* published March 26. Married April 3; New York and Westport, Conn. *Flappers and Philosophers* published. "May Day"; "Head and Shoulders"; "The Camel's Back"; "Bernice Bobs Her Hair"; "The Ice Palace"; "The Offshore Pirate."

1921   Europe May–June; Montgomery; St. Paul. Frances Scott Fitzgerald born in October.

1922   *The Beautiful and Damned* and *Tales of the Jazz Age*. St. Paul and Great Neck, Long Island. "The Diamond as Big as the Ritz"; "Winter Dreams."

1923   *The Vegetable* published; play failed.

1924   Europe. "Absolution"; " 'The Sensible Thing.' "

1

1925	Europe. *The Great Gatsby.* Met Hemingway.
1926	Europe. *All the Sad Young Men.* Began new novel. "The Rich Boy."
1927	Hollywood. At "Ellerslie" near Wilmington, Delaware.
1928	Summer in Paris. "Ellerslie." Basil stories.
1929	Returned to Europe.
1930	Zelda Fitzgerald's breakdown; Switzerland. Josephine stories.
1931	Returned to America; Montgomery; Fitzgerald's second Hollywood job. "Babylon Revisited."
1932	At "La Paix" near Baltimore, Maryland. "Crazy Sunday." Zelda Fitzgerald published *Save Me the Waltz.*
1933	Baltimore.
1934	*Tender is the Night* published.
1935	Zelda Fitzgerald at Highland Hospital, Asheville, N.C. Fitzgerald in Asheville and Baltimore. *Taps at Reveille* published.
1936	Asheville. "The Crack-Up" articles in *Esquire.*
1937	Hollywood. Met Sheilah Graham. Worked for MGM 18 months.
1939	Began *The Last Tycoon.*
1940	Pat Hobby stories. Died, December 21.
1941	*The Last Tycoon* (with *The Great Gatsby* and stories).
1945	*The Crack-Up. The Viking Portable F. Scott Fitzgerald.*
1948	Zelda Fitzgerald died in a fire at Highland Hospital.
1950-51	The Fitzgerald revival. Schulberg, *The Disenchanted;* Mizener, *The Far Side of Paradise;* Kazin, *F. Scott Fitzgerald: The Man and His Work; The Stories of F. Scott Fitzgerald;* revised *Tender Is the Night.*
1957	*Afternoon of an Author.*
1958	Graham, *Beloved Infidel. Fitzgerald Newsletter* (until 1968).

1962   *The Pat Hobby Stories.*

1963   *The Letters of F. Scott Fitzgerald.*

1965   *Thoughtbook of Francis Scott Key Fitzgerald; Apprentice Fiction of F. Scott Fitzgerald, 1909-1917.*

1967   Graham, *College of One;* Bryer, *The Critical Reputation of F. Scott Fitzgerald.*

1969   *Fitzgerald/Hemingway Annual.*

1970   Milford, *Zelda.*

F. Scott Fitzgerald

My Generation

In 1918 the present writer stole an engine, together with its trustful engineer, and drove two hundred miles in it to keep from being A.W.O.L. He can still be tried for the offense, so the details must remain undisclosed. It is set down here only to bear witness to the fact that in those days we were red-blooded—*Children! Don't bring those parachutes into the house!* All right, we'll drop that approach altogether.

We who are now between forty and forty-five were born mostly at home in gaslight or in the country by oil lamps. Mewling and burping unscientifically in our nurses' arms we were unaware of being the Great Inheritors—unaware that, as we took over the remnants of the crumbled Spanish Empire, the robe of primacy was being wrapped around our little shoulders. About ten million of us were born with the Empire, and in our first Buster Brown collars we were treated to a new kind of circuit parade, a Wild West Show on water—the Fleet was being sent on a trip to show

Reprinted from *Esquire,* LXX (October 1968), pp. 119-21, by permission of Harold Ober Associates, Inc. Copyright © 1968 by Frances Scott Fitzgerald Smith. First published in *Esquire* magazine.

the world. At the turn of the previous century—in 1800—it had likewise been bracing to be an American, but that was from ignorance, for beyond our own shore we were a small potato indeed. This time, though, there was no doubt of it—when even our nursery books showed the last sinking turrets of Cervera's fleet we were incorrigibly a great nation.

We were the great believers. Edmund Wilson has remarked that the force of the disillusion in *A Farewell to Arms* derives from Hemingway's original hope and belief. Without that he could not have written of the war: ". . . finally only the names of places had dignity. . . . Abstract words such as glory, honor, courage or hallow were obscene beside the concrete names of villages, the numbers of roads, the names of rivers, the numbers of regiments and the dates." Hemingway felt that way in 1918. In 1899 when he was born there was faith and hope such as few modern nations have known.

It is important just when a generation first sees the light—and by a generation I mean that reaction against the fathers which seems to occur about three times in a century. It is distinguished by a set of ideas, inherited in moderated form from the madmen and the outlaws of the generation before; if it is a real generation it has its own leaders and spokesmen, and it draws into its orbit those born just before it and just after, whose ideas are less clearcut and defiant. A strongly individual generation sprouts most readily from a time of stress and emergency—tensity, communicated from parent to child, seems to leave a pattern on the heart. The generation which reached maturity around 1800 was born spiritually at Valley Forge. Its milk was the illiterate letters, the verbal messages, the casualty reports written during the desperate seven-year retreat from Massachusetts to the Carolinas—and the return back to the Virginia town; its toys were the flintlock in the corner, the epaulettes of a Hessian grenadier; its first legend the print of Washington on the schoolroom wall. It grew up to be the hard-boiled generation of Andrew Jackson and Daniel Webster, Fulton and Eli Whitney, Lewis and Clark. Its few authors, Washington Irving and James Fenimore Cooper, struggled to give America a past, a breathing record of those who had known its forests and fields and towns, a special service for its dead.

They were tougher and rougher than their fathers; they were adrift in a land more remote from the mainstream and all their doubt clothed them in desperation. They revived the duel, long moribund in England. They had a mess on their hands—Washington had died with more apprehension for the republic than he had felt at the lowest ebb of the revolution, and the forces of the time gave life a restless stamp. In retrospect the men seem all of one piece. When the last of them, old General Winfield Scott, watched a new tragedy begin at Bull Run there could have been few men alive to whom he could speak the language of his broken heart.

In haste let me add that my generation is very much alive. One of us recently married Hedy Lamarr!

II

We were born to power and intense nationalism. We did not have to stand up in a movie house and recite a child's pledge to the flag to be aware of it. We were told, individually and as a unit, that we were a race that could potentially lick ten others of any genus. This is not a nostalgic article for it has a point to make— but we began life in post-Fauntleroy suits (often a sailor's uniform as a taunt to Spain). Jingo was the lingo—we saw plays named *Paul Revere* and *Secret Service* and raced toy boats called the *Columbia* and the *Reliance* after the cup defenders. We carved our own swords whistling, *Way Down in Colon Town*, where we would presently engage in battle with lesser breeds. We sang *Tease Me, Coax Me, Kiss Me Good Night, Dear Love,* and *If You Talk in Your Sleep Don't Mention My Name* (which, due to the malice of some false friends, was Fitzboomski all through the Russo-Japanese war). We made "buckboards" out of velocipede wheels and didn't get a page in *Life* about it, and we printed our own photographs in fading brown and blue. The mechanical age was coming fast but many of the things we played with we made ourselves.

That America passed away somewhere between 1910 and 1920; and the fact gives my generation its uniqueness—we are at once prewar and postwar. We were well-grown in the tense Spring of 1917, but for the most part not married and settled. The peace found us almost intact—less than five percent of my college class were killed in the war, and the colleges had a high average compared to the country as a whole. Men of our age in Europe simply do not exist. I have looked for them often, but they are twenty-five years dead.

So we inherited two worlds—the one of hope to which we had been bred; the one of disillusion which we had discovered early for ourselves. And that first world was growing as remote as another country, however close in time. My father wrote the old-fashioned "s" in his youthful letters and as a boy during the Civil War was an integral part of the Confederate spy system between Washington and Richmond. In moments of supreme exasperation he said, "Confound it!" I live without madness in a world of scientific miracles where curses or Promethean cries are bolder—and more ineffectual. I do not "accept" that world, as for instance my daughter does. But I function in it with familiarity, and to a growing extent my generation is beginning to run it.

III

What are these men who, about the time of their majority, found themselves singing, "We're in the army now." Their first discovery of 1919 was that nobody cared. Cut out the war talk—every so often life was doomed to be a cockeyed and disorderly business. Forget quickly.

All right then. Hank McGraw, who had been a major in France, came back to Princeton and captained a winning football team—I never saw him play without wondering what he thought about it all. Tommy Hitchcock, who had escaped from Germany by jumping from a train, went up to Harvard—perhaps to find out why. The best musician I ever knew was so confused that he walked out to put shirts on girls in the Society Islands! Men of fifty had the gall to tell us that when their cellars were exhausted they would drink no more—but they had fixed it so *we* could start with rotgut right now. Most of us took a drink by that time but honestly it wasn't our invention—though both moonshine and heavy necking, which had spread up from the Deep South and out of Chicago as early as 1915, were put upon our bill.

The truth was that we found the youth younger than ourselves, the sheiks and the flappers, rather disturbing. We had settled down to work. George Gershwin was picking out tunes between other peoples' auditions in Tin Pan Alley and Ernest Hemingway was reporting the massacres in Smyrna. Ben Hecht and Charlie MacArthur were watching the Chicago underworld in bud. Dempsey, scarred in reverse by the war, was becoming the brave of his day, while Tunney bided his time. Donald Peattie was coming into his inheritance of the woods and what he found there. George Antheil's music and Paul Nelson's suspended house were a little way off, but Vincent Youmans already had charmed his audience with "O me, O my, O you." Merian Cooper would fly a little longer as a soldier of fortune before settling down to make *Chang* and *Grass*. Denny Holden wasn't through with war either—in his plane last summer perished a gallant and lively jack-of-many-trades whose life was a hundred stories.

The late Tom Wolfe left the Norfolk shipyards and went to college for more education. His end was so tragic that I am glad I knew him in carefree and fortunate times. He had that flair for the extravagant and fantastic which has been an American characteristic from Irving and Poe to Dashiell Hammett. He was six feet eight inches tall and I was with him one night on Lake Geneva when he found to his amazement that not only could he reach the street wires over his head but that when he pulled them he caused a blackout of Montreux. To the inquiring mind this is something of a discovery, not a thing that happens every day. I had a hard time getting Tom away from there quickly. Windows opened, voices called, there were running footsteps, and still Tom played at his blackout with the casualness of a conductor ringing up fares. We drove over the French border that night.

Wolfe was a grievous loss. With Hemingway, Dos Passos, Wilder and Faulkner he was one of a group of talents for fiction such as rarely appear in a single hatching. Each of these authors created a world quite his own and lived in it convincingly. Decimated Europe had nothing to set beside the work of these young men.

The poets of my time set a more precarious course, or so I believe, for the novel had become elastic enough to say almost anything. But some of the critics, Wilson, Mumford, Seldes among others, have had powerful influence upon the taste and interests of the past two decades. The playwrights, Sherwood and Behrman, Barry and Stallings, Hecht and MacArthur, have been so successful that they are now their own angels—contemplating a production, they call for the private sucker list, and find their own names at the top. And that art which stockholders, producers and public have kept in its perennial infancy owes a great debt to those two directors, Frank Capra and King Vidor, who have fought themselves free of producer's control.

All in all it was a husky generation. Match me Tommy Hitchcock or Bill Tilden for sheer power of survival as champions. Outside of a few Eastern cities there was a vacant lot in every block and I played humbly on the same teams with future Minnesota linemen, a national golf medalist, Dudley Mudge, and a national amateur champion, Harrison Johnston.

Later, pursued from hideout to hideout by the truant officers, I came in early contact with a few incipient men of letters. I was at prep school in New Jersey with Pulitzer Prizeman Herbert Agar and novelists Cyril Hume and Edward Hope Coffey. Hope and I were destined to follow a similar pattern—to write librettos at Princeton, "drool" for the college comic and, later, college novels. But I remember him best when he was center and I was quarter-back on the second team at school. We were both fifteen—and awful. There were a couple of one-hundred-eighty-pound tackles (one of them now headmaster for his sins) who liked to practice taking me out, and Hope gave me no protection—no protection at all—and I would have paid well for protection. We were the laziest and lowest-ranking boys in school.

In college I was luckier. I knew the future presidents of many banks and oil companies, the Governor of Tennessee, and among the intellectuals encountered John Peale Bishop, warbird Elliott Springs, Judge John Biggs and Hamilton Fish Armstrong. Of course I had no idea who they were, and neither did they, or I could have started an autographed tablecloth. Things were stirring: Richard Cleveland, Henry Strater and David Bruce led a revolt against the "social system." Spence and Pumpelly and Charlie Taft did the same at Yale.

Next on my list I find Al Capone, born in 1899—but he saw the light in Naples. Anyhow, it's a good place to stop.

John O'Hara

Introduction to *The Portable F. Scott Fitzgerald*

A little matter of twenty-five years ago I, along with half a million other men and women between fifteen and thirty, fell in love with a book. It was the real thing, that love. As one who tries to avoid the use of simile and metaphor, I cannot refrain here from comparing my first and countless subsequent meetings with that book to a first and subsequent meetings with The Girl. You meet a certain girl and you say to yourself, in the words of a 1928 song, "How long has this been going on?" The charm has to be there from the very beginning, but then you see that this time it is more than charm (although charm can be enough). The construction, of book or girl, has to be there from the very beginning, but then you see that this time it is more than the construction (although construction can be enough in the case of the girl). Well, not to hack away at the point too long or often, I took the book to bed with me, and I still do, which is more than I can say of any girl I knew in 1920.

After the appearance of that book I was excitedly interested in almost anything that was written by F. Scott Fitzgerald; his novels, short stories, and his nonfiction articles. He was born in September 1896 and I got here in January 1905, both of us just for the ride, but in spite of the at that time very important difference in our ages I regarded him as one of us. He knew what we were talking about and thinking about, if you could call it thinking, and what he knew was every bit as true of us who were of Earth '05 as of the '96 codgers.

The novel was *This Side of Paradise*. It is not included in this volume. Mrs. Parker did not consult me in making her selections for this volume, and it is only my job to write an introduction. I have no quarrel with her selections, either. Get that straight. Within the limitations of space she has brought together a truly representative collection, and please bear in mind not only that these words of mine are an introduction to this book, but that this book itself will turn out to be an introduction: an introduction to Scott Fitzgerald for the pleasure of those who haven't had the pleasure. This may not have been the publishers' or Mrs. Parker's intention, but I am fairly certain that it's going to work out that way.

Cantering along on that assumption, we can take first things first, and so, in book-jacket language, a word about the author. He would have been fifty next year, but if ever a man was not meant to be fifty, it was Fitzgerald. I don't mean that he tried as hard as Ernest Hemingway not to be fifty. Most of his life Ernest Hemingway has followed the big shooting as doggedly as Mr. Morgan used to go after the Scottish grouse, whereas Fitzgerald never heard a military shot fired in anger. Fitzgerald in his way, though, did go into battle, and when you read about the beating of Dick Diver by the Italian Fascist bums in *Tender Is the Night* you will see what I mean. Scott was ever one to like thinking of himself as a man of action and I commit no libel when I say he could be quarrelsome. The last time I talked to him he telephoned me—we were both in California—to ask me to serve as his second in a duel. A Hollywood trade paper had blasted a girl whom Fitzgerald admired. He wanted to fight a duel with the editor of the paper, and it seemed to me that if Scott won a duel with that editor he would be doing no disservice to the Hollywood community, but, stalling for time, I pointed out that under the code duello, as I understood it, the challenged and not the challenger had the choice of weapons. "I'm sure he's no better with foils or sabers than you are," I said, "but he may be a damn sight better shot."

"I didn't say anything about shooting," said Scott. "I'm just going in his office and beat the hell out of him, and I want you to come along so the rest of his bastards don't jump me."

I had a type-louse's-eye view of the two of us going to that print shop, pushing past the receptionist, and Scott taking the editor apart, which I honestly think he could have done. The two men were about the same weight and height, Scott was a bit younger than the editor, and he had Righteous Wrath and a Lady's Kerchief on his side. But I couldn't see the editor's goons standing idly by during this performance, and I couldn't see myself doing a William Farnum to a succession of Tom Santschis. Hot lead can be almost as effective coming from a linotype as from a firearm. I therefore attempted Reason. I told Scott that it was a laudable enterprise he had in mind, but pointed out to him that he would be doing the lady no good, that he was a married man with a daughter in college in the East, and that if he went storming into a "newspaper" office and we had a brawl in defense of a lady's honor we would just make the first pages of the early editions of practically every afternoon paper in the land—not to mention the Paris edition of the *New York Herald Tribune* and *Time* magazine. The notoriety would be notoriety and nothing else; if you kill a cop, all cops hate you; if you thrash a newspaper man all newspaper men except his immediate competitors hate you, and the stories that would appear would not be very understanding about his defense of the young lady in question.

"In other words, you're saying no," said Fitzgerald.

"If you insist on going, I'll go with you, but I don't want you to go and I don't want to go with you."

"That's all I wanted to know," he said. "I thought you were my one real friend in this town. I'll get Eddie —. He's diabetic and he doesn't get into fights, but he's a gentleman."

He hung up.

He was telephoning from a place where he had to call through the operator, so I immediately dialed Eddie, who was a friend of mine, and told him what to expect. The strange thing was that Scott did not telephone Eddie, who sat in his room all morning preparing arguments against Scott's project. Maybe Scott realized that what I said made sense; he surely knew instinctively without my telling him; and maybe he was actually counting on me as a friend to talk him out of the assault and battery (with intent to kill). Who knows? But I do know this much: although that was Spring and Scott didn't die until December, he never telephoned me again.

The above sad little anecdote could be matched or bettered by any of the men and women whom Scott knew and loved best: Dorothy Parker, Robert Benchley, Maxwell Perkins, Charles Mac-Arthur, Hemingway, Gerald and Sara Murphy, Edith Wharton, Edmund Wilson, John Dos Passos, Ring Lardner, and Harold Ober; the Princeton pals whom he would suddenly remember after ten or twenty years and even boys who had gone to Newman, the lace-curtain Catholic prep school which he attended; the beauty and talent of Hollywood in the Twenties; the beauty and talent and corruption of the Riviera in the Twenties and Thirties; the favorite barkeeps everywhere; the Curb & Snaffle set in Maryland and Long Island; the casual pick-ups between Santa Barbara and St. Jean de Luz whom Scott would invest with something or other they didn't quite have, but who for a while would think they had it—whatever it may have been—all along, and which Scott would let them have whenever he thought of them. He never really lost track of anybody. The first man I ever met who knew Scott Fitzgerald was a trying snob who had been in Scott's class at Princeton, who came to my dinky home town for a Winter Assembly because the girl who asked him hadn't been able to sew up the captain of the Yale football team. Ten years later, when I was getting to know Fitzgerald pretty well, I mentioned the fellow. Scott hadn't seen him since my meeting, but Scott knew enough about his marital, social, and economic progress to make you think they were seeing each other all the time. Mind you, Scott didn't like him, never had, and hadn't known him well in college, but it was characteristic of Scott to be a sort of class secretary, except that the class included—at my guess—50,000 men and women. I have a pastime, which is to read *Who's Who*, and I am up on a large number of persons whom I haven't met, don't expect to meet, and don't particularly want to meet. With Scott it was something more; contributing an anecdote or a physical description or some scandal, success, or failure.

This predilection of Scott Fitzgerald's could easily have been confusing to him in his work. I imagine that part of the time he would find himself writing about people he knew, but frequently he must have had the sometimes doubtful pleasure of meeting a person whom he had once created for a story. The one was as real as the other. His work had that all the time: verisimilitude, reality, truth. This was true even when he took exercises in fantasy, a line of endeavor which usually bores me, because I haven't the patience and whatever other equipment is essential to the understanding of symbolism. He always knew what he was writing about, which is so, so untrue of so, so many so-so writers. It may not seem like much in 1945, when it is done all the time, but twenty-five years ago it was delightful to find a writer who would come right out and say Locomobile instead of high-powered motor car, Shanley's instead of gay cabaret, and George, instead of François, the *chasseur* at the Paris Ritz. These touches guaranteed that the writer knew what he was talking about and was not getting his information from Mr. Carnegie's local contribution to culture. The reader usually knew, without stopping to think much about it, that if a family owned a Franklin it was because they didn't feel they could afford a Pierce-Arrow. A prejudice persists among some eye-weary souls who are professional book critics that men's clothes, for instance, are not worthy of description. I can think of one fellow, for instance, who used to earn his living at book criticism but is now a sort of radio announcer, who used to suffer terribly when Brooks Brothers was mentioned. And yet if a writer were to put the fellow into Brooks Brothers clothes you would recognize him right away for a spy. If, as is most unlikely, the same critic knew about guns, I can imagine his shrieks at the luckless, careless writer who would confuse a Webley with a Savage, or if boats were being discussed, let the writer make a mistake about a suit of sail and the whole work would be suspect. And properly. This particular ex-reviewer doesn't, however, know much about clothes, and there are photographs to prove it. Scott Fitzgerald had the correct impressions because, quite apart from his gifts, the impressions were not those of a man who's never been there. As we used to say, he knew the forks.

It is a dangerous thing to bother about the rich. A writer who does it in this country—at least during and since the times when barbers and bootblacks were piling up fabulous fortunes of from five to forty thousand dollars—will find himself regarded as a toy. The professional pipe-smokers—chiefly book critics and editorial writers—could understand *The Great Gatsby* because who couldn't? Too, Fitzgerald put one over in that book; he made the important rich man seem like an unimportant heel, and Gatsby, a man who happened to have a lot of money but was not a rich man, was made so pitiable that there were those who loved him. In the story frankly called "The Rich Boy" you get a four-reel motion picture of a rich man, in Technicolor, but the pipe-smokers never made much comment on that one, probably because it was a short story and they didn't have the name of O. Henry or Maupassant to identify it. But in two novels which dealt with the rich, Fitzgerald gave them, the rich, the business, yet the choice of those novels appearing in this volume was snooted by the conservative press no less than by the liberal and leftist. I was annoyed, but I don't recall having been surprised. In this country the rich don't write; there are really so few of them, and they can't write anyway. Americans who write, and those who write criticism, almost without exception are of middle-class origin no matter whom they write for or what they write, the *Wall Street Journal* or the *Daily Worker*. They have very little contact with the rich or none at all. The exceptions are the small number of men who get to know the rich at Yale, Harvard, or Princeton. Nowhere else. The rich don't go to other colleges. The rich I mean are the kind of people who can say, "If you have to ask how much a yacht will cost, you can't afford it." You give a thought to how few men get to know the rich in college, and how few of *them* become writers, and you will see why there is very little accurate writing about the rich, and you will see why there are no critical standards for dealing with the rich, and why the public will just as readily accept, oh, say, Louis Bromfield or Edna Ferber as it will Scott Fitzgerald. About the public I am not really complaining. An artist is his own fault. But a critic who passes judgment on a novel by Frederick Prokosch or the Shangri-La book—or for that matter, a novel about share-croppers—ought to be curious and careful and conscientious enough to be something besides casually contemptuous of a work of art. To wit: *Tender Is the Night.*

But Scott wasn't only a man who better than anyone else wrote about the rich. Actually most of his work was about the middle class, your family and mine. And in this book there is a short story called "Absolution" which shows he left the Plaza Hotel on occasion.

Yes, he had a place in American Literature. Scott Fitzgerald had a place in American Literature. Somewhere between Arthur Dwight Croveney and the Deep Blue Sea? All he was was our best novelist, one of our best novella-ists, and one of our finest writers of short stories. The dynamite money goes to other authors, one of whom I am sure was given her cheque for $46,000 and her Chinese visa with all the unlimited grace at Fitzgerald's command. To a now rather grumpy playwright went another 46 G's for his somewhat less than indigenous observation of the American scene. To a third American author, the same sum, complete with medal, for his capable christening of a character who culturally set us back a fast fifty years, because a lot of people were satisfied to be that character. Possibly it is not gracious of us Americans to refrain from establishing a ten-million-dollar fund to pass judgment on Swedish letters, Swedish being just as tough as American. And yet you look in an old *World Almanac* and re-examine the awards handed out by the trustees of Columbia University and it might strike you that Gothenburg—the one that is not in Nebraska—is at least as close to home as is Morningside Heights. Gothenburg and Morningside have in common no mention of F. Scott Fitzgerald.

The custom, which I intend to follow, is to compare the artist with his contemporaries. Hemingway was more of a contemporary of Fitzgerald's than Sinclair Lewis. Still, Lewis and Fitzgerald were writing about the same times, while Hemingway, good and influential as he was, wasn't using the same material. Fitzgerald and Lewis were covering the same ground at the important time, but it's funny to read the two men on the same subject. Lewis, then, and Lewis right this minute, is King of the Corn—and by way of being the Sweetheart of it. The names that Lewis dreams up are as improbable as those you will find in *The Chronicles of Clovis* or *The Unbearable Bassington*. Lewis now is accepted as a satirist when it can be devoutly doubted that he was trying to be anything but a commenter on the American scene. It always has seemed to me that one day Lewis woke up to find himself called a satirist, and became one by continuing to play straight. Fitzgerald was no satirist. Not even in *The Great Gatsby*. If he was being a satirist, as has been claimed, I don't get it, and I am no dope. He burlesqued—not too broadly, since it wasn't necessary—the squandering of money on Long Island in Prohibition days, it's a fact he did. That wasn't being satirical; that was only a slight heightening for the ultimate effect of showing for all time one very sad man who was, except for his love and death, an ass, and I wish I could go further and tell you what animal I am thinking of. (You put a saddle on the animal.) No, my friend, Fitzgerald had more than satire to offer. The satire was implicit for all to see, just as a writer's politics are there for anyone to see who has the curiosity and intelligence to wonder. Politically, Scott was an anarchist, as is anyone who is not a Fascist or a religious Communist. He never said he was cynical of all the governments and all the governing; it was just there to be seen. He never wore a badge saying, "Tee-hee, I'm a satirist."

I speak of Sinclair Lewis, who, of course, is Johnny One-Note. This fact remains a 33rd degree secret from the Nobel and Pulitzer judges, who patiently regard the American male as something between Will Rogers and the roles best played by Walter Huston. Come down heavy on your r's, don't dress Eastern, be a tall-size hypocrite, and your creator automatically wins half the heavy-weight prize. Remember, too, if you are the author, that the female sex is to be handled in pasture, once over lightly. Any other treatment just shows how you stand on the question of virility. Fitzgerald didn't feel that way, act that way, or write that way. Fitzgerald could believe that an American man and woman were capable of married love, and that if a husband heard the call of the wild it wasn't inevitably toward the direction of a plump, inexperienced organist or a plump, bored woman in a hotel with a funny quasi-Indian name. For a man who has always been around and who periodically takes an austerely moral stand (curiously reminiscent of Rollin Kirby's Prohibition cartoons), Sinclair Lewis has some strange ideas about the sack-time of American men. On the subject of extra-legal love you will come across two sentences by Fitzgerald the like of which are not available in any Lewis that I recall. They read: "For a long time afterward Anson believed that a protective God sometimes interfered in human affairs. But Dolly Karger, lying awake and staring at the ceiling, never again believed in anything at all." Even without reading the story ("The Rich Boy") is there anything wrong or much lacking in that? Not to be too rough on Lewis, give him his due: he can write about bank buildings and receptacles for used razor blades and he can almost approximate the speech of an un-witty Abe Martin and he can make you remember that George F. Babbitt's middle initial stood for Follinsbee, but he hasn't put down a man or a woman who is the real thing. God knows I have encountered thousands of Babbitts, but I don't believe in Sinclair's particular George.

Who else is there who might be considered a professional contemporary of Fitzgerald's? Hemingway I will not discuss while
there is a war on, for he writes best between wars and I think his
best work already is familiar to many readers to whom this book
really will be a Fitzgerald introduction. Who else? I honestly don't
think of anyone else. The collegiate material was handled by Cyril
Hume and Cornell Woolrich and Katharine Brush and Percy
Marks and Stephen Vincent Benét and Lynn and Lois Montross,
but who among the new Fitzgerald audience would know whether
Benét wrote *The Wife of the Centaur* or *The Beginning of Wisdom?* There is even a strong possibility that only Benét's name
among them would have a familiar sound. If I were to get on the
squawk-box and say to Fighting 18: "Now hear this: Carl Van
Vechten is aboard and will be pleased to answer any questions"—
would the fighter pilots know what the hell to ask him? I hardly
think so, but when you have read this book you might care to
know that Van Vechten's slim volumes (*The Blind Bow Boy, The
Tattooed Countess, Nigger Heaven*) had a little of the same screwy
life that was caught by Fitzgerald in *The Great Gatsby*. A minor
but sharp talent called Jack Thomas produced a pleasant little
item called *Dry Martini*, but I myself haven't read that since
Thomas died, which was almost fifteen years ago. Most certainly
other writers were at their scrivening in the twenty years of
Fitzgerald. The only trouble is I can't think of them without doing
the kind of digging that I am postponing until I start bucking
M.A., which must wait until I get my bachelor's, which must wait.

Notwithstanding his sure place as an American writer, it was
a happy circumstance that Fitzgerald was not a lit'ry figure. He
was not a literary-tea boy (none of the good ones are), and more-
over his readers, the greater number of them, were people who
could take a book or leave it alone. He was an artist and at the
same time enough of an artisan to sell stories to *The Saturday
Evening Post* and still say what he wanted to say. "Babylon Revisited" appeared in the *Post* while George Horace Lorimer, not
exactly an *erotica* man, was boss. Except for a small part of the
revelation of the incestuous relationship between Nicole and her
father, *Tender Is the Night* was first serialized in the old *Scribner's*. He wrote a lot for the magazines without an ignominious
amount of compromise. It goes without saying that all who read
him in the *Post* did not buy his books, just as it goes without say-

ing that all who bought his books did not take as gospel or even as ultimate entertainment every word he wrote. But he *was* a *popular* writer. He reached an astonishing number of people who spent not half as much money on books as they did on golf balls or lingerie clasps. Those who were old, and those already committed to being old, never got around to him as they did take to Louis Bromfield, say, who was around Fitzgerald's age and who also was around in Fitzgerald's era. What is to be hoped for with this collection is a new and enormous and appreciative audience not unlike in joy of discovery the Sherlock Holmes fans who came along many years after Doyle had put a stop to Holmes. In my generation (I am forty) and among men and women now in their fifties can right now be found a good-sized number who are able to compare notes on Fitzgerald's work without quite going so far as the Holmes fans, who form clubs and go to their meetings by hansom cab and wear deerstalker caps. That is how real Fitzgerald character and incident have become to many of us. I go to the Plaza Hotel two or three times a week, not with any genuine expectation of running into Paula Legendre or Scott Fitzgerald. You will find a few pages on that Paula died in childbirth, and you already know that Scott is dead. And yet, last week, during those exhaustingly hot days, I saw Anson over and over again, sometimes in uniform and sometimes not. And last year I saw a pregnant girl who could have been Paula Legendre. And always, without fail, whether I'm going to the Plaza for a haircut or a drink (or even to talk over the arrangements covering this Introduction) I am half prepared to see Scott himself. He was elusive in life, God knows, and all through the writing of this piece he has refused to stay put, but the ectoplasm or the artist need not bother the reader or even me. For after all the *stuff* is here. The stuff is very much here, and it's mellow.

Long Island, July 23, 1945.

John Kuehl

Scott Fitzgerald's Critical Opinions

Scott Fitzgerald wrote for money more bad fiction than any other American of similar stature. He deeply regretted this. In 1924 he told Edmund Wilson, "I really worked hard as hell last winter—but it was all trash and it nearly broke my heart."[1] In a letter to John Peale Bishop, he observed, "I've done about 10 pieces of horrible junk in the last year tho that I can never republish or bear to look at" (CU, pp. 267-68). Nor was he ever happy about his experiences in Hollywood, where he found turning out "movie" scenarios even more trying than writing pot-boilers for magazines. Although the cinema was "the greatest of all human mediums of communication,"[2] it "was no art, . . . [it] was an

Reprinted from *Modern Fiction Studies*, VII (Spring 1961), 3-18, by permission. *Modern Fiction Studies*, © 1961, by the Purdue Research Foundation, Lafayette, Indiana.
[1] Wilson, Edmund (ed.), *The Crack-Up* (New York, 1956), pp. 264-65. *N.B.* Hereafter designated CU.
[2] The F. Scott Fitzgerald Papers, Princeton University Library, Princeton, New Jersey, Fitzgerald to his daughter, Frances Scott Fitzgerald, Winter, 1939. *N.B.* Unless otherwise indicated, the Papers are the source of subsequent letters. Following the first reference to a correspondent, he or she is specified by initials. Dates are frequently listed in abbreviated form. The

industry."[3] In one of his "Pat Hobby" stories (short satirical sketches about life in Hollywood), Pat remarked, "They don't want authors. They want writers—like me."[4]

When on May 20, 1940, Fitzgerald told Max Perkins that he "just couldn't make the grade as a hack" because this kind of performance required "a certain practised excellence" which he did not possess, he was underrating himself. Despite his lack of success in Hollywood, his commercial fiction shows that as a slick writer he was well above average. He maintained otherwise because he wanted to think of himself as an artist and not merely as a writer-for-hire like the fictitious Pat Hobby. That as an artist he approached his serious works, his "labors of love," with intelligence and perception is clear from the literary criticism embedded in the letters, some of the published canon and other sources.

I

Scott Fitzgerald laid great stress upon the writer's need of self-conscious *craft*. On March 4, 1938, he commented to Mr. Dayton Kohler:

> Some people seem to look on our time as a sort of swollen Elizabethan age, simply crawling with geniuses. The necessity of the artist in every generation has been to give his work permanence in every way by a safe shaping and a constant pruning, lest he be confused with the journalistic material that has attracted lesser men.

The intensity with which he held the conviction that form and economy are essential to good writing is well illustrated in his attitude toward Thomas Wolfe.

The fact that the latter was neither a "shaper" nor a "pruner," interested neither in form nor economy, was the basis of Fitzgerald's view of his work. Wolfe poured himself out; he cultivated "every stray weed found in the garden." The real artist, the craftsman, must be selective:

---

reader will notice that sometimes I have quoted letters and Notebooks directly from the originals in the Fitzgerald Papers and that sometimes I have relied upon *The Crack-Up* as my source. Besides other reasons, too numerous and complicated to explain here, this method was employed to facilitate research.

[3] "Boil Some Water—Lots of It," *Esquire*, XIII, No. 3 (March, 1940), 30.

[4] "Mightier Than the Sword," *Esquire*, XV, No. 4 (April, 1941), 181.

That is where talent comes in to distinguish between the standard blooms which everyone knows and are not particularly exciting, the riotous and deceitful weeds, and that tiny faint often imperceptible flower hidden in a corner which, cultivated a la Burbank is all it will ever pay us to cultivate whether it stays small or grows to the size of an oak. (to Morton ——, 8/3/39)

Wolfe marshaled his material in a "gawky and profuse way" (to Mrs. Bayard Turnbull, 3/15/35) and as a result was only "half-grown artistically."[5] In his copy of *Of Time and the River* Fitzgerald wrote in the margin, "All this has been about as good as Dodsworth for chapter after Chapter," and "trite, trite, trite, trite, page after page after page." In reply to Fitzgerald's advice that he try to be a more conscious artist, Wolfe said, "A great writer is not only a leaver-outer but also a putter-inner," citing Shakespeare, Cervantes and Dostoevsky as evidence (CU, p. 314). This did not mitigate Fitzgerald's antagonism toward the sprawling novel. Nevertheless, he had to admit that with all his faults Wolfe had not committed "the cardinal sin" of writing a work that did not continue "to live" (to FSF, 11/29/40).

Wolfe was not the only American writer who neglected craftsmanship. Scott Fitzgerald felt that most Americans were guilty of this and that the reason for their neglect was an obsession with material rather than style. In the article "How to Waste Material," he wrote:

Ever since Irving's preoccupation with the necessity for an American background, for some square miles of cleared territory on which colorful variants might presently arise, the question of material has hampered the American writer. For one Dreiser who made a single-minded and irreproachable choice there have been a dozen like Henry James who have stupid-got with worry over the matter, and yet another dozen who, blinded by the fading tail of Walt Whitman's comet, have botched their books by the insincere compulsion to write "significantly" about America.

He went on to say that even now, when a usable past has been discovered and "the foundations have been laid," American writers are still more interested in subject matter than craft. They write about the American farmer, American cities, American politics,

---

[5] The F. Scott Fitzgerald Papers, the "Literary" section of the Notebooks. *N.B.* Hereafter designated LSNB.

business, society, and because this is a "literary gold rush," they
have no time to be artists. The material is "turned out raw and
undigested." Two men, Fitzgerald believed, shared the responsibility for the current manifestations of this long-existing American
literary sickness. One was H. L. Mencken, whom he praised for
himself but condemned for his influence on young authors. Because Mencken had "always been ethical rather than aesthetic,"
he had "begotten a family of hammer and tongs men—insensitive,
suspicious of glamor, preoccupied exclusively with the external,
the contemptible, the 'national' and the drab." The other was
Sherwood Anderson who, because he had been misinterpreted, had
been imitated as a man of ideas rather than a writer with a brilliant style. But there was hope. Now that Ernest Hemingway had
published *In Our Time*, a book Fitzgerald had read with more
interest than any since Conrad, American letters were looking up.
Instead of serving up "raw food" from "the railroad restaurants of
California and Wisconsin," Hemingway cultivated a prose in which
"there is not a bit to spare." Fitzgerald implied his own position
when he said: "Material, however closely observed, is as elusive as
the moment in which it has its existence unless it is purified by an
incorruptible style and by the catharsis of a passionate emotion."[6]

Scott Fitzgerald's style shows "shaping" or "a molding of the
confusion of life into form,"[7] and "pruning" or economy. These are
well exemplified in the painstaking way he cut and revised his
material. Even in *This Side of Paradise*, inferior in art to his later
work, he tells us he "wrote and revised and compiled and boiled
down."[8] From *The Great Gatsby* he deleted enough to make
another novel,[9] but was still dissatisfied. He complained to Bishop
that he had not reached the stage of "ruthless artistry which would
let me cut out an exquisite bit that had no place in the context"
(CU, p. 271). *Tender is the Night*, composed between 1925 and
1934, went through three versions and numerous titles. Fitzgerald
once remarked that he had written more than 400,000 words on
it, but had thrown away three-fourths.[10] Even after its publication
he labored over it, finally deciding that the story should be pre-

---

[6] *The Bookman*, LXIII, No. 3 (May, 1926), 262-65.

[7] "The Bowl," *The Saturday Evening Post*, January 21, 1928.

[8] "Who's Who: F. Scott Fitzgerald," *The Saturday Evening Post*, September 18, 1920, p. 61.

[9] Introduction to the Modern Library edition, 1934.

[10] Malcolm Cowley, Introduction to *Tender is the Night*, *Three Novels of
F. Scott Fitzgerald* (New York, 1953), p. iv.

sented in chronological order rather than beginning as in the original version with Rosemary meeting the Divers and their circle. But although Scott Fitzgerald revised his work with considerable care, often making several drafts before arriving at the one he wanted, he tried not to overwrite. In a letter of January 17, 1938, to Joseph Mankiewicz, he said that his kind of style could not survive excessive reworking, and in his "Notes" to *The Last Tycoon* he reminded himself: "Rewrite from mood. Has become stilted with rewriting. Don't look. Rewrite from mood."[11]

Fitzgerald had a healthy respect for the single word and the single line. He once said that a single word could change the emphasis and the value in a scene or setting (to Bennett Cerf, 8/13/36). The "best . . . instance of artistic power," he wrote of Grace Flandrau's *Being Respectable,* was "the remarkable portrait of Valeria": "We have scarcely a glimpse of her, and she says only one line throughout. Yet the portrait is vivid and complete."[12] In spite of the drastic revisions in his novels, he did not throw away anything that he considered good. He went through the stories that he did not intend to republish in a book, took out the best phrases and passages, had his secretary enter these in his Notebooks, and then marked the stories "stripped" and not to be published again. Later, these same phrases and passages turned up in his novels. He felt similarly about the significance of scenes. He wrote to Bishop on January 30, 1935: "I could tell you plenty of books in which the main episode, around which swings the entire drama, is over and accomplished in four or five sentences." A scene's importance was not to be measured by its length.

Fitzgerald confessed that he had been accused of a "fatal facility" in his early work and that subsequently he "labored like a slave over every sentence so as not to be like that."[13] His goal was "to develop a hard, colorful prose style" (to FSF, 1937). He achieved it, but how? For one thing, he used verbs whenever possible instead of adjectives:

> About *adjectives:* all fine prose is based on the verbs carrying the sentences. They make sentences move. Probably the finest

---

11 *Ibid.,* p. 134.
12 *The Literary Digest International Book Review,* I, No. 4 (March, 1923), 36.
13 "Afternoon of an Author," *Esquire,* VI, No. 2 (August, 1936).

technical poem in English is Keats' *Eve of Saint Agnes.* A line
like:

> The hare limped trembling through the frozen grass, is so alive
> that you race through it, scarcely noticing it, yet it has colored
> the whole poem with its movement—the limping, trembling, and
> freezing is going on before your own eyes. (CU, p. 303)

He wrote natural sentences. In one of his letters, he remarked:

> People don't begin all sentences with *and, but, for* and *if,* do they?
> They simply break a thought in mid-paragraph, and in both
> *Gatsby* and *Farewell to Arms* the dialogue tends that way. Stick-
> ing in conjunctions makes a *monotonous* smoothness. (to JM,
> 1/17/38)

He avoided stilted language. Instead of such phrases as " 'pitched
forward,' " which Edmund Wilson used in one of his short stories,
Fitzgerald advised colloquialisms like " 'sorta sank down' " (CU,
p. 263). Because Wilson and Bishop were over-careful, they did
not achieve "the queer slanting effect of the substantive, the
future imperfect, a matter of intuition or ear to O'Hara" (LSNB).
Fitzgerald's style appealed to the senses. He observed Conrad's
definition of writing—to make the reader hear, feel, and above all
else, see. In *McTeague*, by appealing "to the sense of smell or of
hearing rather than by the commoner form of word painting,"
Frank Norris had given an air of authenticity.[14]

A critic of others, Fitzgerald desired, even encouraged, sincere
and detailed criticism from people whom he respected. In reference
to a review Bishop was going to write on *The Beautiful and
Damned,* he said: "Tell specifically what you like about the book
and don't. . . . I'm so afraid of all the reviews being general" (CU,
p. 258). If he felt criticism justified, he accepted it graciously. For
example, he told Bishop that he had learned something from his
comments on *The Great Gatsby* in spite of the fact that they had
caused him pain (CU, p. 275). Often he was his own severest
critic. He admitted that *Gatsby* had a serious fault, namely that
he had not known or accounted for the feelings between the hero
and Daisy from the time of their reunion to the end (CU, p. 270).

---

[14] Review of *Brass,* by Charles Norris, *The Bookman,* LIV, No. 3 (November, 1921), 253-54.

By 1938 no one was harsher about *This Side of Paradise* than the author himself.

II

Along with craftsmanship—shaping and pruning—poetry and originality were essential for the development of a great style. Scott Fitzgerald had heard poems from his father's lips at an early age. This and his conviction that "the talent that matures early is usually of the poetic, which mine was in large part" (to FSF, 7/18/40), helps to explain the fact that much of his early writing was verse.[15] But despite his success in having "The Way of Purgation" accepted by *Poet Lore* in 1917, Fitzgerald, through Amory in *This Side of Paradise*, confessed that he would "never write anything but mediocre poetry" because he was "not enough of a sensualist" and noticed only "obvious things."[16] Fitzgerald was quite right about his poetry. Only occasionally is the magic we often find in his prose revealed in his verse. For the most part, it is undistinguished and dull. Nevertheless, his feeling for poetry was in large measure responsible for the beauty of his prose style. "Poetry," he wrote to his daughter on August 3, 1940, "is either something that lives like fire inside you—like music to the musician or Marxism to the communist—or else it is nothing." Once he informed her that he did not believe a person could write "succinct prose" without first attempting an "iambic pentameter sonnet" and reading Browning's short dramatic monologues (CU, p. 304). On another occasion (7/29/40) he warned her that her own style lacked distinction and that the way to achieve it was to "cultivate your own garden," which could be done only through poetry, "the most concentrated form of style."

Originality was of the utmost importance, Scott Fitzgerald believed. The inventor, he declared, was "infinitely superior" to those who simply did things well; for example, Giotto or Leonardo was greater than Tintoretto and D. H. Lawrence than John Steinbeck (CU, p. 294). The prose talent depended upon "having something to say and an interesting, highly developed way of saying it" (to FSF, 7/18/40). Once (1/30/35) he advised Bishop to eliminate "all traces of other people." In Bishop's *Act of Darkness*, Fitz-

---

[15] Fitzgerald's first published poem was "Football," which appeared in *Newman News* in 1911.
[16] New York, Charles Scribner's Sons, 1920, p. 93.

gerald thought there were patterns "which derived background from Hemingway." Bishop should delete these passages "no matter how satisfactory" they were and acquire something that was more himself. Fitzgerald admitted in the same letter that he had had to fight this battle too, no doubt referring to the year-and-a-half during which he deliberately stopped reading Hemingway because he feared the latter's rhythms were replacing his own.

The young writer should ignore "the known, the admired and the currently accepted" as well as that false voice within that tells him that his feelings and actions are not universal, interesting, or right. Instead he should listen to that true voice within that "makes him write down those apparently exceptional and unimportant things" because they are "his style, his personality— eventually his whole self as an artist" (to M, 8/3/39). Yet the young writer can do certain things that the older writer cannot afford to do. It was natural for Thomas Wolfe to make a chapter in *Look Homeward Angel* almost a parody of the first chapter of *Ulysses* and for Fitzgerald to be imitative in *This Side of Paradise*. However, if this becomes a habit, the writer will lose all chance of developing a personality (to JPB, 1/30/35). Then, too, the early novel may be formless because "the lack of a pattern gives the young novelist more of a chance to assert his or her individuality, which is the principal thing."[17]

Besides studying poetry, "the most concentrated form of style," in order to develop originality, the young artist should read other writers. Fitzgerald recommended that he "absorb half a dozen top flight authors every year." If he does, his style will become "a subconscious amalgam" of all that he has admired. If not, it will be "simply a reflection of the last writer" he has read, "a watered-down journaleese" (to FSF, 7/18/40). This attitude is not a contradiction of his insistence upon eliminating "all traces of other people." He is saying that a good style comes from soaking up many elements, the new concoction being an original; whereas an inferior style results from being influenced by one person exclusively.

Fitzgerald described the kind of author the young artist should study:

---

[17] Review of *The Love Legend,* by Woodward Boyd, *New York Evening Post,* October 28, 1922, sec. 3, pp. 143-44.

If you were learning tennis you would form yourself not upon an eccentric like Tilden, for example, but upon players with classic styles, like Cochet or La Coste (my references are of the dim past). You cannot imitate a mannerism with profit; a man might labor over Tilden's tennis style for six years, finding at the end that it simply couldn't be done without Tilden's 6'6" in height. (to M, 8/9/39)

In the same letter he went on to enumerate some of the "great English classics": *A Farewell to Arms, Dubliners,* "The Eve of St. Agnes," "Ode on a Grecian Urn," *Huckleberry Finn, Daisy Miller* and "The Drums of the Fore and Aft." But since these English classics tend to be more eccentric than the French, which are "the most *classical* classics," the young writer might profit more by reading something like Maupassant's "Maison Tellier." In any event, he should spend his time studying good things. On July 29, 1940, Fitzgerald reminded his daughter that after she had read Gertrude Stein's "Melanctha," she sold a *New Yorker* story, but when she was reading the average novel, she sank back "to a Kitty-Foyle-Diary level of average performance."

Scott Fitzgerald was convinced that he himself had achieved originality. On one occasion he said that people could read his stamp "blind like brail" [*sic*] (LSNB) and he wrote to Perkins (5/20/40): "Even now there is little published in American fiction that doesn't slightly bare [*sic*] my stamp—in a *small* way I was an original."

But achieving originality would not have been possible had Fitzgerald not had something to say. Having something to say is essential to finding a way of saying it. Indeed, in the creative artist, Fitzgerald insisted, style and subject matter become one:

Nobody ever became a writer just by wanting to be one. If you have anything to say, anything you feel nobody has ever said before, you have got to feel it so desperately that you will find some way to say it that nobody has ever found before, so that the thing you have to say and the way of saying it blend as one matter—as indissolubly as if they were conceived together. . . .

Let me preach again for a moment: I mean that what you have felt and thought will by itself invent a new style, so that when people talk about style they are always a little astonished at the newness of it, because they think that it is only *style* that they are talking about, when what they are talking about is the attempt to express a new idea with such force that it will have the originality of the thought. (CU, pp. 303-304)

Although novels are not written with the idea of creating a philosophical system, the novelist must have "a sharp and concise attitude about life."[18] He did not, however, write merely because he wanted to say something; on the contrary, he wrote because he had something to say (CU, p. 123). Scott Fitzgerald felt that the writers in his time did not have sharply defined attitudes toward life or diversified material. Joseph Conrad had avoided this by being brought up "in a metier utterly unrelated to literature" (CU, p. 301). Thomas Wolfe, on the other hand, had not escaped. Fitzgerald said of him: "His awful secret transpires at every crevice—he did not have anything particular to say! The stuff about the GREAT VITAL HEART OF AMERICA is just simply corny." Wolfe had recapitulated what Whitman, Dostoevsky, Nietzsche, and Milton had said before him, but "unlike Joyce and T. S. Eliot and Ernest Hemingway," he had "nothing really new to add." This was because he had failed to find "a solid gold bar like Ernest's courage, or Josef Conrad's art or D. H. Lawrence's intense cohabitations"; instead, he had told us what we already knew, that everything was a "mess" and that it was "too bad about the individual" (to FSF, 11/29/40).

But even better authors, perhaps because they have found "a solid gold bar," do not have a limitless stock of themes. Most men have only "two or three great and moving experiences" in their lives—"experiences so great and moving that it doesn't seem at the time that anyone else has been so caught up and pounded and dazzled and astonished and beaten and broken and rescued and illuminated and rewarded and humbled in just that way before." Even though they believe when they find "a new background and a novel twist" that they have departed from their two or three tales, they are actually repeating them. This is not wholly bad because without this they would have "no individuality at all."[19] However, these themes, regardless of what they are, cannot be merely reported; rather, the author must express "the *profound*

---

18 Introduction to the Modern Library edition of *The Great Gatsby,* 1934.
19 "One Hundred False Starts," *The Saturday Evening Post,* March 4, 1933, pp. 13, 65-66.

essence of what happened" so that "even a forlorn Laplander" may *"feel* the importance of a trip to Cartier's!" (CU, p. 304). Nor is it permissible to depart from reality. The author must illustrate that same "desire to imitate life which is in all the big shots" (LSNB). He has another responsibility too. He must help the reader all he can with most of his observations, clothing only his "more radical" ideas in "sheep's wool" (to V. F. Calverton, 11/4/36).

III

Besides his convictions about the elements that compose a great style, there are at least two other important aspects of Fitzgerald's views on writing: the place of morality and the role of "subjectivity" and "objectivity."

It must have come as a surprise to Scott Fitzgerald's early contemporary readers who thought of him chiefly in connection with *This Side of Paradise,* which "shocked" with its apparently frank exposé of youthful manners and morals, to discover later that Fitzgerald was a highly "moral" author. Indeed, he has frequently been called "a spoiled priest," the term he used to describe Dick Diver in his "Notes" on *Tender is the Night,* the same term, incidentally, with which James Joyce once referred to Stephen in *Ulysses.* Fitzgerald considered himself a moralist, as certainly he was. He tells us that he had "a New England conscience—developed in Minnesota"[20] and that in spite of his opposition to schoolteachers, there was "just the ghost of one in me" (to Mrs. BT, 10/20/35). Most revealing is a comment from a letter of 1939: "I guess I am too much a moralist at heart, and really want to preach at people in some acceptable form, rather than to entertain them" (CU, p. 305). Without attempting here to analyze the morality in Fitzgerald's work, let me briefly examine two or three typical attitudes showing him to be a moralist.

In his Notebooks Scott Fitzgerald said that his "stamp" was "taking things hard" and in a letter of July 5, 1937, to his daughter that "despite a tendency to self indulgence" he had "some essential seriousness" that would manage to preserve him. It comes as no surprise then to find him saying of the post-war period that "living wasn't the reckless, careless business these people thought."

---

20 *Ibid.*

America might be headed for "the greatest, gaudiest spree in history," but Fitzgerald, for one, could not share its naive optimism. All the plots he thought of "had a touch of disaster in them." He anticipated that lovely girls would go to ruin, that wealth would disintegrate, that millionaires would be "beautiful and damned" (CU, p. 87). In 1917 he had stated that although epicureanism had been "romantic" in his early days at Princeton, it was "rather disgusting in the city" because "it was much too easy; it lacked the penance of the five o'clock morning train back to college."[21]

Lionel Trilling once observed that Fitzgerald's work is "innocent of mere 'sex.' "[22] This resulted from the fact that as a romanticist he based relations between men and women on mental and spiritual rather than physical needs while some of his contemporaries, particularly the naturalists, stressed only physical attraction. Fitzgerald felt that " 'sex books,' . . . arouse pruriency and sometimes . . . kill the essence of romance."[23] He did not approve of vulgarity. On August 13, 1936, he wrote to Bennett Cerf that he would like to eliminate the line in *Tender is the Night* "I never did go in for making love to dry loins" because it was "definitely offensive." On another occasion he said that he would have found the "streak of vulgarity" in an unspecified Hemingway book "quite offensive" had he not known that Hemingway deliberately used it "as a protest against censorship" (to Alice Lee Myers, 9/29/32). All this, of course, does not mean that Scott Fitzgerald was a prude. He was simply opposed to vulgarity for vulgarity's sake. He was also opposed to hypocrisy in these matters. For example, he considered the novel *Simon Called Peter* a "piece of trash" because "the characters move in a continual labyrinth of mild sexual stimulation" over which "the colored lights of romantic Christianity" played. But Sherwood Anderson's *Many Marriages* was not immoral. It was "the reaction of a sensitive, highly civilized man to the phenomenon of lust."[24] Fitzgerald was against Puritanism in any form. As an anti-Philistine, he took an intense dislike to any group of "professional uplifters." He said that the Philadelphia Society, for example, possessed a "depressing

---

[21] "The Spire and the Gargoyle," *Nassau Literary Magazine,* LXXII, No. 7 (February, 1917).
[22] Kazin, Alfred (ed.), *F. Scott Fitzgerald: The Man and His Work* (Cleveland and New York, 1951), p. 197.
[23] An article with no title, *New York American,* February 24, 1924, p. LII-3.
[24] Review of *Many Marriages,* by Sherwood Anderson, *New York Herald,* March 4, 1923, sec. 9, p. 5.

conviction of sin" and that it appealed "to the intellect of farmers' wives and pious drug-clerks."[25]

Fitzgerald disliked censorship too. When William Woods, Editor of *The Literary Digest*, asked for his opinion, he replied (4/19/ 23):

> The clean book bill will be one of the most immoral measures ever adopted. It will throw American art back into the junk heap where it rested comfortably between the *Civil War* and *The World War*. The really immoral books like *Simon Called Peter* and *Mumbo Jumbo* won't be touched—they'll attack Hergeshiemer [sic], Drieser [sic], Anderson and Cabell whom they destest [sic] because they can't understand. George Moore, Hardy and Anatole France who are unintelligable [sic] to children and idiots will be suppressed at once for debauching the morals of village clergymen.

Later he expressed a similar opinion of the "halfwitting halfwit Hayes and his legion of decency." Although he had urged his daughter not to see the moving pictures of 1932-33 "because they were suggestive and salacious," now that the Hayes group wanted to interfere with *"all* strong themes" so that the only safe films were either "feeble and false" or dealt "with children," he went to the other extreme (CU, p. 303).

His "Notes" to *The Last Tycoon* effectively illustrate Scott Fitzgerald's concern about instilling a moral into his stories. He says that Monroe Stahr's plane will crash and as had actually happened in an incident of 1933 the bodies of the dead will be rifled, but this time by three children. One boy, Jim, is to steal Stahr's possessions; Dan is to rifle the body of a ruined producer, Bradogue; and a girl, Frances, will rifle the body of an actress. The belongings they find, which reflect the character of the dead passengers, will determine the attitude of the children toward the theft. Frances, like the actress, will become selfish; Dan, like the unsuccessful producer, will become irresolute; but Jim, who has identified himself with Stahr, will redeem them by confessing the crime. Jim, therefore, will turn out "all right," while Frances, who has been corrupted, may become "anything from a gold digger to a prostitute," and Dan, whose morals have been completely demolished, will from this time forward always try "to get something

---

[25] "The Claims of the Lit.," *Princeton Alumni Weekly,* March 10, 1920, p. 514.

for nothing." Since Fitzgerald is an artist as well as a moralist, he insists that his lesson be presented unobtrusively. Of Dan's new resemblance to Bradogue, he says: "This must be subtly done and not look too much like a parable or moral lesson, still the impression must be conveyed, but be careful to convey it once and not rub it in. If the reader misses it, let it go—don't repeat." At the end of the episode, he says:

> I cannot be too careful not to rub this in or give it the substance or feeling of a moral tale. I should [show] very pointedly that Jim is all right and end perhaps with Frances and let the readers hope that Frances is going to be all right and then take that hope away by showing the last glimpse of Frances with that lingering conviction that luxury is over the next valley, therefore giving a bitter and acrid finish to the incident to take away any possible sentimental and moral stuff that may have crept into it.[26]

Like Keats, Scott Fitzgerald struggled between "objectivity" and "subjectivity," and, again like Keats, he was primarily a "subjective" writer. After his death, several American critics began to take this dualism into account. John Dos Passos called his work "a combination of intimacy and detachment" (CU, p. 342); Malcolm Cowley, "a sort of double vision."[27] But, however they phrased it, the critics agreed that it was the author's ability to participate in his fiction and at the same time to stand aside and analyze that participation that gave his work maturity and power. This is best illustrated by *The Great Gatsby*, where, to a great extent, the author acts as Gatsby and observes as Nick. Since this "double vision" is very important to Scott Fitzgerald's work, no review of his critical opinions can afford to overlook it.

Fitzgerald copied into his Notebooks Keats's statement that "men of genius" do not have "any individuality and determined character" (CU, p. 95), which agrees with another remark in the Notebooks, namely that there has never been "a good biography of a good novelist" because "he is too many people if he's any good" (LSNB). But perhaps the most telling comment Fitzgerald made on "objectivity" is the following:

> Books are like brothers. I am an only child. Gatsby my imaginary eldest brother, Amory my younger, Anthony my worry. Dick my

---

26 *Three Novels of F. Scott Fitzgerald*, pp. 141, 157-58.
27 Kazin, p. 148.

comparatively good brother but all of them far from home. When I have the courage to put the old white light on the home of my heart, then—(LSNB)

Since on September 14, 1940, he told Gerald Murphy that *The Last Tycoon* was "as detached from me as *Gatsby* was, in intent anyhow," he might well have added Monroe Stahr to his list.

But although Fitzgerald valued the aspect of detachment in his work and came to use it with considerable skill, he was more concerned about the "subjective" approach to art. This was true because romanticist as he was, he felt self-revelation to be one of the most vital components of creativity:

> I used to think that my sensory impression of the world came from outside. I used to actually believe that it was as objective as blue skies or a piece of music. Now I know it was within, and emphatically cherish what little is left. (to GM, 3/11/38)

Fitzgerald opposed the tendency to psychoanalysis that was growing in his period. It caused the disintegration of personality and "the extinction of that light is much more to be dreaded than any material loss" (to John O'Hara, 7/25/36). Since everything he had written was himself (to Harold Ober, 7/19/39), so much so in fact that he was not able to remember when he wrote anything because he had "lived in [the] story" (LSNB), any technique that would tend to destroy self would also destroy the springs of art.

Scott Fitzgerald, as I have already mentioned, felt that the young writer must listen to that voice within that encourages him to record his feelings and actions because these feelings and actions are actually "his style, his personality—eventually his whole self as an artist." Developing individuality is so very important that it is natural for the young writer to begin with a formless novel; the lack of pattern will give him a chance to exploit his selfiess. If he starts with emotions that are close to him and that he can understand, eventually he will evolve two or three major themes. These become his "stamp." If he feels them strongly enough, he will automatically present them in a new way. Thus it is that the artist creates a vision of life, a vision of utmost value to other men:

> The genius conceives a cosmos with such transcendental force that it supersedes in certain sensitive minds, the cosmos of which they

have been previously aware. The new cosmos instantly approximates ultimate reality as closely as did the last.[28]

Someone once said—and I am quoting most inexactly—"A writer who manages to look a little more deeply into his own soul or the soul of others finding there, through his gift, things that no other man has ever seen or dared to say, has increased the range of human life." (to M, 8/3/39)

To a greater extent than he was perhaps aware, Scott Fitzgerald solved the conflict between "objectivity" and "subjectivity." In a letter of November 9, 1938, to Miss Frances Turnbull, he tells her that he has read her story but that "the price for doing professional work is a good deal higher" than she is willing to pay. The writer must sell his "heart," his "strongest reactions," and not just minor things that he "might tell at dinner." This pertains especially to beginning writers who "have not yet developed the tricks of interesting people on paper," who, because they lack technique, "have *only* . . . emotions to sell." He gives examples:

It was necessary for Dickens to put into Oliver Twist the child's passionate resentment at being abused and starved that had haunted his whole childhood. Ernest Hemingway's first stories "In Our Time" went right down to the bottom of all that he had ever felt and known. In "This Side of Paradise" I wrote about a love affair that was still bleeding as fresh as the skin wound on a haemophile.

When the amateur sees the professional take "a trivial thing such as the most superficial reactions of three uncharacterized girls and make it witty and charming," he believes that he can do likewise. But, at that stage, he does not possess the professional's ability "to transfer his emotions to another person" in a skilful and subtle way; the amateur can effect this transfer only "by some such desperate and radical expedient as tearing your first tragic love story out of your heart and putting it on pages for people to see." Since, therefore, the admission price to a writing career is high, and often conflicts with one's "attitude on what is 'nice,'" the neophyte will have to decide whether or not he is willing to make the necessary sacrifices. Talent is only "the equivalent of a soldier

---

[28] Review of *Many Marriages*.

having the right physical qualifications for entering West Point";
self-revelation is the other essential ingredient.

This letter is interesting on two counts: first, it demonstrates
Fitzgerald's conviction that all writers, beginners and veterans,
inevitably exploit their own emotions and experiences; second, it
shows the development that came about in both his novels and his
critical opinions. Whereas the beginning writer, because he lacks
technique may simply describe everything in a more or less direct
way, the professional, because he has gained knowledge in living
and technique in writing, is able to *transfer* to something or someone outside himself his deepest or most trivial feelings. In other
words, subject matter is always highly personal, but while it remains merely personal to the young writer, the mature artist finds
ways of projecting it objectively. This, of course, implies T. S.
Eliot's "objective correlative."

Scott Fitzgerald's career as an artist followed very closely his
observations to Miss Turnbull. All his work is subjective, reflecting
his own experiences and emotions, but the early novels present
these in quite a direct way, while the later work employs two
devices—"composite" character and the sympathetic, intelligent
observer—to transfer them to something or someone outside the
author.

In *This Side of Paradise* the love affair between Amory and
Isabelle is a fairly faithful rendition of Fitzgerald's own love affair
with Ginevra King, which was "still bleeding as fresh as the skin
wound on a haemophile." Monsignor Darcy is almost an exact
replica of Monsignor Fay, a good friend of Fitzgerald during his
college days, whose letters, Fitzgerald tells us, were transcribed in
the book with practically no changes.[29] The autobiographical material in *The Beautiful and Damned* was also presented, by and
large, directly. A comment the author made to his daughter on
June 14, 1940, however, shows us that at the time he was writing
this novel, he was groping for greater "objectivity":

> Gloria was a much more trivial and vulgar person than your
> mother. I can't really say there was any resemblance except in the
> beauty and certain terms of expression she used, and also I natu-
> rally used many circumstantial events of our early married life.

---

[29] Fitzgerald Papers, Fitzgerald's letter of February 26, 1921, to Frances
Newman in his copy of *Frances Newman's Letters.*

However the emphases were entirely different. We had a much better time than Anthony and Gloria had.

Jay Gatsby, Dick Diver, and Monroe Stahr were all "composite" characters. Gatsby "started out as one man I knew and then changed into myself—the amalgam was never complete in my mind" (CU, p. 271). But Gatsby was not only the author and Max Fleischman; he was also "perhaps created on the image of some forgotten farm type of Minnesota" (to John Jamieson, 4/15/34). Dick Diver and his wife, Nicole, were based to some extent on Sara and Gerald Murphy, friends of Zelda and Scott Fitzgerald. But when Hemingway complained that the latter had tampered with them, changed them into something different, something they were not in real life, he was unconsciously paying tribute to Fitzgerald's artistic development. He answered Hemingway (6/1/34) by reminding him that before he had ever attempted "composite characterization" the "feat of building a monument out of three kinds of marble" had been "brought off" by no less a person than William Shakespeare. It was all right, then, for Dick and Nicole to be himself and Zelda as well as the Murphys. Monroe Stahr was Scott Fitzgerald but he was also the Hollywood producer Irving Thalberg. "Composite" characters, characters that were an amalgamation of himself and other people, gave "objectivity" to the author's later novels in two ways: they were outside their creator and therefore could reflect his emotions and experiences by indirection rather than immediately; since they were a combination of the author and other persons, they reflected not solely the author's emotions and experiences, but their own as well.

The observer as narrator was the second important technique Fitzgerald acquired in his efforts to achieve greater "objectivity." When the story-teller is someone other than the author, an aesthetic distance is created between the characters under observation and the author, a distance resulting from the story-teller's acting as a sort of middle man. Thus Fitzgerald was forced to take into consideration not only his reactions, but the reactions of the "persona" who represented man in general almost as much as he did his creator. The device, which came to Fitzgerald chiefly through his study of Joseph Conrad's Marlow, is responsible for the feeling of greater "objectivity" in *The Great Gatsby* and *The Last Tycoon* as compared with *Tender is the Night,* where the writer himself is the all-knowing narrator.

We may well believe his daughter when she tells us that "sweat," "heart-breaking effort," and "painful hours of work under the most adverse circumstances" made Scott Fitzgerald's finest prose possible.[30]

[30] Frances Scott Fitzgerald (Lanahan), "Princeton and F. Scott Fitzgerald," *Nassau Literary Magazine,* C, No. 3 (Hundredth-Year Issue, 1942), 45.

John Kuehl

Scott Fitzgerald's Reading

Most American critics, from the publication of *This Side of Paradise* in 1920 through the Fitzgerald revival in the 40's and 50's, agreed that Scott Fitzgerald, though possessed of a great natural talent, was lacking in intellectual ability. In 1925 Edmund Wilson said: "He has been given imagination without intellectual control of it; he has been given a desire for beauty without an æsthetic ideal; and he has been given a gift for expression without many ideas to express."[1] Two decades later Alfred Kazin wrote that Fitzgerald's "actual intelligence was never equal to his talent."[2] Arthur Mizener declared in 1949 that Fitzgerald "had almost no capacity for abstract ideas or arguments."[3] Malcolm Cowley went further in 1951: "He was not a student, for all the books he read; not a theoretician and perhaps one should flatly say, not a thinker."[4] Ten years earlier Glenway Wescott had been even more drastic: "Aside from his literary talent—literary genius, self-taught—I think Fitzgerald must have been the worst educated man in the world."[5]

Reprinted from *The Princeton University Library Chronicle*, XXII (Winter 1961), 58-89, by permission of the journal. © The Princeton University Library.

One critical voice alone was raised in opposition to this chorus of disparagement. In 1950 Lionel Trilling stated:

> It is hard to overestimate the benefit which came to Fitzgerald from his having consciously placed himself in the line of the great. He was a "natural," but he did not have the contemporary American novelist's belief that if he compares himself with the past masters, or if he takes thought—which, for a writer, means really knowing what his predecessors have done—he will endanger the integrity of his natural gifts.[6]

I agree with Mr. Trilling's analysis, feeling, as he did, that Scott Fitzgerald had "intellectual courage," a "grasp . . . of the traditional resources available to him," a "connection with tradition and with mind," and propose, therefore, in the pages that follow, to demonstrate its rightness by examining as closely as possible the author's reading.[7]

Fitzgerald had some knowledge of classical language (Latin)[8] and literature (Greek and Latin) from his school and college training. At Newman he studied Latin grammar, Latin composition, Caesar, Cicero, and Vergil, courses in which he received D, B, E, C, and D respectively.[9] At Princeton he took Latin 103, 104, 203, and 204, earning Group 5, 5, 5, and 6. Although he made passing references to several of the standard Greek and Latin authors and was probably familiar with such works as *The Iliad* and *The Odyssey*, the Greek dramas, the complete Plato, *The Golden Sayings of Epictetus*, Petronius Arbiter's *Satyricon*, Plutarch's and Suetonius' *Lives*, he was apparently no fonder of the classics than he was capable of mastering them.[10] He once said that a course in Greek civilization and literature "seems to me a profound waste of time,"[11] and in a poem of 1916, appropriately entitled "To My Unused Greek Book," he wrote:

> Thou still unravished bride of quietness,
> Thou joyless harbinger of future fear,
> Garrulous alien, what thou mightst express
> Will never fall, please God, upon my ear.[12]

Only one "classic" evoked much enthusiasm from Scott Fitzgerald. As was the case with many other novelists and poets of the 1920's, he responded to the more "literary" portions of the Bible, espe-

cially Ecclesiastes. In regard to the latter, he cautioned his daughter: "Remember when you're reading it that it is one of the top
pieces of writing in the world."[13]

Like the classics, the literature of the European Renaissance did
not particularly stimulate Fitzgerald. Although he mentioned
Dante and Montaigne and knew at least *The Decameron*,[14] *Don
Quixote, Gargantua and Pantagruel* and the poems of François
Villon, he had nothing significant to say about either the authors
or their achievements.

The English Renaissance, on the other hand, had a slight but
important effect on him. He called Shakespeare "whetting, frus-
trating, surprising and gratifying"[15] and once commented: "Despite Mr. Taine, in the whole range from Homer's Oddysey [*sic*]
to Master's [*sic*] idiocy, there has been but one Shakespeare."[16]
Fitzgerald was probably more interested in Shakespeare's songs
and sonnets than he was in the plays, for among the volumes he
gave to Miss Graham only *King Lear* is heavily marked while he
checked carefully five sonnets and twelve songs.[17] He was familiar
as well with the work of Chaucer, Wyatt, Spenser (*The Faerie
Queene*), Sidney, Lodge, Drayton, Marlowe, Dekker, Donne, Jon-
son, Herrick, Waller, Milton (*Paradise Lost*; "L'Allegro"), Suck-
ling, Crashaw, and Marvell ("To His Coy Mistress"). Here is one
of the many reading lists he sent to his daughter:

> Since you've finished the "Farewell To Arms" the second bit of
> reading includes only the following poems. The reference is to the
> index of first lines in either the Oxford Book or the Golden
> Treasury.
>
> | Come Unto These | Shakespeare |
> | Tell Me Where | " |
> | Hark, Hark the Lark | " |
> | Take Oh Take | " |
> | Go Lovely Rose | Waller |
> | Oh Western Wind | Anon |
> | Art Thou Poor Yet | Dekker |
> | Fear No More | Shakespeare |
> | My True Love | Sidney |
> | Who Is Sylvia | Shakespeare |
>
> The question will be along about *Wednesday*. If you read these
> ten poems you can answer it in a flash.[18]

Clearly, Fitzgerald was drawn to the lyrical aspect of English
Renaissance literature. This, of course, is consistent with his love

for "pure" poetry in general, a lifelong love that unquestionably affected his prose style.

Since the lyric note was almost absent in the eighteenth century, one is not surprised to find that with the exception of *Moll Flanders*, which he thought of as a masterpiece,[19] Benjamin Franklin's *Almanac*, and Edward Gibbon's *The Decline and Fall of the Roman Empire*, this period made practically no impression on him.[20]

Because of the resurgence of lyricism in the work of the romantic poets, one is equally well prepared to learn that the early nineteenth century was the first era, chronologically speaking, to influence Fitzgerald extensively.[21] He had at least a nodding acquaintance with Chatterton, Blake, Burns, Scott, Coleridge, Landor, and Hood; he was fond of Wordsworth's poems, especially "Ruth," "A Slumber Did My Spirit Seal," "Elegiac Stanzas: Peele Castle"; and he recommended in one of the two surviving reading lists he composed for Miss Graham a number of Shelley pieces which she was to study in conjunction with André Maurois' *Ariel*.[22] The other list, as its heading indicates, concerns Byron:[23]

Suggestions about Byron

The excerps [*sic*] from long poems are short because of the fine print. I have never been able to admire but five or six of his short lyrics in comparison to his contemporaries.

After Chap 2[24] read	*The Isles of Greece*	Ox. p. 565	
After Chap 4 "	*Childe Harold*	Works	
	Canto III, Stanzas 21-28		
After Chap 5 "	*Maid of Athens*	Works p. 59	
After Chap 7 "	*So We'll go no more*	}	Ox p. 564
	She Walks in Beauty	}	Ox p. 564
After Chap 8 "	*Don Juan, Canto one*	Works	
	CXIII to CXVII		
After Chap 10 "	*Don Juan Canto Two*	} Works	
	CLXXII-CLXXVII	}	
	and Canto Eleven LX	}	
At End "	*Once More: The First 3 Stanzas of*		
	"The Isles of Greece"		

But John Keats was Fitzgerald's favorite author. He provided Miss Graham with Sidney Colvin's *Life* and a *Works* in which he singled out several titles.[25] "Ode to a Nightingale" was "one of the greatest poems of our language,"[26] and "The Eve of St. Agnes" and

"Ode on a Grecian Urn" were "great English classics."[27] Once he advised his daughter, who recalls that he often went about the house reciting Keats from memory, to take the course "*English Poetry: Blake to Keats*" because "a real grasp of Blake, Keats, etc. will bring you something you haven't dreamed of."[28] In *This Side of Paradise*, Amory "declaimed 'The Ode to a Nightingale' to the bushes they passed"[29]—the same "Ode to a Nightingale" that gave *Tender Is the Night* its name—and Anthony Patch in *The Beautiful and Damned* has "a yellowed illegible autograph letter of Keats's."[30] Just a few months before his death, Scott Fitzgerald wrote:

Poetry is either something that lives like fire inside you—like music to the musician or Marxism to the communist—or else it is nothing, an empty, formalized bore around which pedants can endlessly drone their notes and explanations. *The Grecian Urn* is unbearably beautiful with every syllable as inevitable as the notes in Beethoven's Ninth Symphony or it's just something you don't understand. It is what it is because an extraordinary genius paused at that point in history and touched it. I suppose I've read it a hundred times. About the tenth time I began to know what it was about, and caught the chime in it and the exquisite inner mechanics. Likewise with *The Nightingale* which I can never read through without tears in my eyes; likewise the *Pot of Basil* with its great stanzas about the two brothers "Why were they proud, etc."; and *The Eve of St. Agnes* which has the richest, most sensuous imagery in English, not excepting Shakespeare. And finally his three or four great sonnets, *Bright Star* and the others.

Knowing those things very young and granted an ear, one could scarcely ever afterwards be unable to distinguish between gold and dross in what one read. In themselves those eight poems are a scale of workmanship for anybody who wants to know truly about words, their most utter value for evocation, persuasion or charm. For awhile after you quit Keats all other poetry seems to be only whistling or humming.[31]

It is not surprising, then, that Fitzgerald was attracted to three late nineteenth-century French symbolist poets, Paul Verlaine, Arthur Rimbaud, and Jules Laforgue.[32] Here is a "free translation" of Rimbaud's "Voyelles" ("Vowels") appearing in Miss Graham's copy of *Poésies*:

A black, E white, I red, U green, O blue
vowels

Some day I'll tell where your
  genesis lies
A—black velvet swarms of flies
Buzzing above the stench of voided bowels,

A gulf of shadow; E—where the iceberg
  rushes
White mists, tents, kings, shady strips
I—purple, spit blood, laughter of
  sweet lips
In anger—or the penitence of lushes

U—cycle of time, rythm [*sic*] of seas
Peace of the paws of animals and wrinkles
On scholars brows, strident tinkles
On the supreme trumpet note, peace
of the spheres, of the angels. O equals
X ray of her eyes; it equals Sex.

Of French prose fiction written about this time, he especially admired Maupassant's *La Maison Tellier* and Flaubert's *Madame Bovary*.[33]

In 1932 John Jamieson sent a letter to *Hound & Horn*, taking issue with an essay composed for that magazine by Lawrence Leighton, who had spoken of Flaubert as Fitzgerald's "ultimate master." Many years later, Mr. Jamieson commented to Arthur Mizener on his letter:

In my letter to the *H & H*, I remarked that I thought Fitzgerald owed much more to the extremely personal manner of writing generally used by English and American novelists before the advent of James and Moore, than he did to Flaubert's rigorously impersonal manner. I argued that Fitzgerald "perhaps" owed most of all to "that least impersonal of novelists, Thackeray," and that Nick's reflections in *The Great Gatsby* were used to enrich the texture of the narrative and to focus its dramatic passages rather in the manner of the little essays and asides to the reader in Thackeray's novels. The chapter opening containing the catalogue of Gatsby's guests was cited as an example.[34]

Fitzgerald replied to Mr. Jamieson's "*Hound & Horn* letter," a copy of which he received in 1934:

I was interested also in your analysis of the influences upon my own books. I never read a French author, except the usual prep-

school classics, until I was twenty, but Thackeray I had read over
and over by the time I was sixteen, so as far as I am concerned
you guessed right.[35]

But this is not the only statement that indicates his awareness of
a debt to Thackeray. Corresponding with John Peale Bishop on
the same day, Fitzgerald observed:

> On receiving your first letter with its handsome tribute and
> generous praise I realized that I had been hasty in crediting that
> you would make such a criticism as "this book [*Tender Is the
> Night*] is no advance on *Gatsby.*" You would be the first to feel
> that the intention in [the] two books was entirely different, that
> to promote myself momentarily *Gatsby* was shooting at something
> like *Henry Esmond* wile [*sic*] this was shooting at something like
> *Vanity Fair.* The dramatic novel has cannons [*sic*] quite different
> from the philosophical, now called psychological novel. One is a
> kind of *tour de force* and the other a confession of faith. It would
> be like comparing a sonnet sequence with an epic.[36]

Richard Caramel, the writer in *The Beautiful and Damned*, had
said, "My publishers, you know, have been advertising me as the
Thackeray of America,"[37] and Gertrude Stein had stated in 1925:

> You are creating the contemporary world much as Thackeray did
> his in *Pendennis* and *Vanity Fair* and this isn't a bad compliment.
> You make a modern world and a modern orgy [*sic*] strangely
> enough it was never done until you did it in *This Side of Para-
> dise.*[38]

Samuel Butler was so important to Fitzgerald that Mr. Mizener
considered Butler "his favorite author."[39] Although I cannot agree
with this conclusion, there is no question about Fitzgerald's enthusiasm. Anthony of *The Beautiful and Damned* "had recently
discovered Samuel Butler and the brisk aphorisms in the notebook
seemed to him the quintessence of criticism." Speaking from his
own person, Fitzgerald characterized these same *Note-Books* as
"the most interesting human document ever written,"[40] and went
so far as to compile a set for himself using Butler as his model—
(unfortunately, they are what he termed them, "a leather-bound
waste-basket,"[41] some of the entries of which not even he could
decipher).

Fitzgerald's other reading of English writers in the Victorian period was so extensive that it must be confined to a note,[42] while our discussion cites only a few relatively significant facts, comments, and markings.

In an undated letter to his daughter, he observed, "I don't think anyone can write succinct prose unless they have at least tried and failed to write a good iambic pentameter sonnet, and read Browning's short dramatic poems, etc.—but that was my personal approach to prose," and in Volume II of the *Poems and Plays* of Robert Browning which he gave to Miss Graham, he checked eleven works.[43] Among the lyrics of Swinburne, under whose spell (as well as that of Rupert Brooke) he had composed poetry during 1916 and 1917, he liked best "Atalanta in Calydon," "Laus Veneris," "The Garden of Proserpine," "The Triumph of Time," and "When the Hounds of Spring." He said of the first: "The fullest and most talented use of *beat* in the English language. The *dancingest* poem"; and of the second: "Notice how this influenced Ernest Dowson. In this read only as far as you like. When it was published (1868?) it was a great mid-Victorian shocker." He drew a line after stanza eight of "Laus" with the marginal remark, "The rest is too long."[44] In *Rudyard Kipling's Verse; Inclusive Edition, 1885-1918*, he singled out for Miss Graham more than twenty poems, and in her copy of *Puck of Pook's Hill*, he called attention to six stories.

Fitzgerald's comments in another of her books, *Essays in Criticism, Second Series* by Matthew Arnold, are especially meaningful in view of his vision of himself as "a spoiled priest":

> Fitzgerald (p. 100): "Later ages have entirely disagreed with this [Arnold's opinions on the initial page of Chapter IV, "John Keats"]. It shows Victorian stiffness and primness in its most unattractive pose."
>
> Arnold (p. 132): "Yet I firmly believe that the poetical performance of Wordsworth is, after that of Shakespeare and Milton, of which all the world now recognises the worth, undoubtedly the most considerable in our language from the Elizabethan age to the present time." Fitzgerald (margin): "This, with its following artillery, is a famous critical sentence. Why it is accepted with such authority is a mid-Victorian mystery. Yet—it has effected [*sic*] everyone. I place Keats above him but I am such a *personal* critic and may be wrong, because of the sincerity of this God damned sentence."

Fitzgerald (p. 133): "Mister Arnold had not read Pushkin— nor seen evidently [*sic*] that Dostoiefski (if he knew him) was a great poet. Later you must compare this essay ["Wordsworth"] with Wilson's in *The Triple Thinkers.*"

Fitzgerald (p. 141): [After quoting the sentence, "Voltaire does not mean, by 'treating in poetry moral ideas,'" and underlining the word, "not"] "You see this is my case against Stienbeck [*sic*] —or rather Mare's case against Zola."

Fitzgerald (p. 142): [After underlining the sentence, "The question, *how to live*, is itself a moral idea"] "This is Arnold at his best. Absolutely without preachment."

Arnold (p. 143): "Poetry is at bottom a criticism of life." Fitzgerald (margin: "a famous line, a fine line."

Fitzgerald (p. 144): "Pretty daring for this old boy!"

Fitzgerald (p. 145): "Now he becomes 'moral'—nevertheless follow him because this is real 'thinking through.'"

Of Dickens' novels, Fitzgerald felt *Bleak House* was the finest and said in regard to *Oliver Twist*: "It was necessary for Dickens to put into Oliver Twist the child's passionate resentment at being abused and starved that had haunted his whole childhood."[45] Of Oscar Wilde's *Dorian Gray*, a work that unquestionably affected *This Side of Paradise*, he remarked later, first in a letter to Max Perkins (April 23, 1938) and second in a letter to his daughter (October 5, 1940):

. . . looking it [*This Side of Paradise*] over, I think it is now one of the funniest books since "Dorian Gray" in its utter spurious- ness. . . .

Dorian Gray is little more than a somewhat highly charged fairy tale which stimulates adolescents to intellectual activity at about seventeen (it did the same for you as it did for me). Sometime you will re-read it and see that it is essentially naive. It is in the lower ragged edge of "literature" just as *Gone With the Wind* is in the higher brackets of crowd entertainment.[46]

It was Scott Fitzgerald's opinion that Dickens, Tennyson, Wilde, and De Musset were writers of the last century who had acquired reputations quickly, "but the reputations of Hardy, Butler, Flau- bert and Conrad were slow growths. These men swam up stream and were destined to have an almost intolerable influence upon succeeding generations."[47]

Among the late nineteenth-century American writers Fitzgerald read, Henry James and Frank Norris warrant individual attention.

More than one critic has felt that he belongs in the Jamesian tradition of the novel. Charles Weir contended that "a progression might easily be established . . . from Henry James to Fitzgerald to John O'Hara,"[48] and T. S. Eliot said that *The Great Gatsby* seemed to him "to be the first step that American fiction has taken since Henry James."[49] Other critics have been more specific. Arthur Mizener tells us that Gilbert Seldes said that *The Great Gatsby* was written in the scenic method which was derived through Edith Wharton from James and intimates that Seldes must have known what he was talking about because he had spoken to Fitzgerald regarding the book. Mr. Mizener further states that Edmund Wilson had been urging Fitzgerald to read James.[50] Since Fitzgerald thought of *Daisy Miller* as one of the "great English classics,"[51] perhaps Malcolm Cowley is right in arguing that Daisy Buchanan was named after James's heroine. He is wrong, however, when he hints that the technique of the single observer came from James.[52] This device was directly inspired by Joseph Conrad.

Actually, one is treading on very unsure ground in making definite connections between James and Fitzgerald because Fitzgerald admired only James's early work. He said of *The Portrait of a Lady*, which is commonly placed at the end of James's "first phase," that it was "in his 'late second manner' and full of mannerisms." He advised his daughter to read *Daisy Miller* or *Roderick Hudson* instead.[53] On another occasion, he referred to "the questionable later stylistics of Henry James."[54] Nor, apparently, was he satisfied with James's approach to material:

> Ever since Irving's preoccupation with the necessity for an American background, for some square miles of cleared territory on which colorful variants might presently arise, the question of material has hampered the American writer. For one Dreiser who made a single minded and irreproachable choice there have been a dozen like Henry James who have stupid-got with worry over the matter. . . .[55]

Scott Fitzgerald became conscious of the realistic-naturalistic movement in native letters when, in 1919, he read C. G. Norris's *Salt*, which he called "a most astounding piece of realism."[56] In 1921 he explained the impact the novel had had on him:

> Although not one of the first I was certainly one of the most enthusiastic readers of Charles Norris's "Salt"—I sat up until five

in the morning to finish it, stung into alertness by the booming repetition of his title phrase at the beginning of each section. In the dawn I wrote him an excited letter of praise. To me it was utterly new. I had never read Zola or Frank Norris or Dreiser— in fact the realism which now walks Fifth Avenue was then hiding dismally in Tenth Street basements. No one of my English professors in college ever suggested to his class that books were being written in America. Poor souls, they were as ignorant as I—possibly more so. But since then Brigadier General Mencken has marshaled the critics in [an] acquiescent column of squads for the campaign against Philistia.[57]

The part Mencken played in introducing him to American naturalism is made clear in *This Side of Paradise*, where Fitzgerald says of Amory that he was

> rather surprised by his discovery through a critic named Mencken of several excellent American novels: "Vandover and the Brute," "The Damnation of Theron Ware," and "Jenny Gerhardt." McKenzie, Chesterton, Galsworthy, Bennet, had sunk in his appreciation from sagacious, life-saturated geniuses to merely diverting contemporaries.[58]

In the words of Henry D. Piper, whose article "Frank Norris and Scott Fitzgerald"[59] is a detailed account of Norris's influence, "It is not surprising to find Fitzgerald enthusiastically proposing to Charles Norris that they do something about bringing out a memorial edition of Frank Norris's collected works, a project which did not actually materialize until more than a half-dozen years later."[60] Charles, Frank's brother and creator of *Salt*, wrote to Fitzgerald on November 15, 1920, "Your suggestion about the special edition of my brother's books appeals but I fear you will not get very much enthusiasm out of D. P. and Co who got 'stung' on an edition of 'Vandover' of 2000 copies."[61] Mencken knew of the proposal also; he commented (probably on October 7, 1920), "The Norris scheme is excellent and it goes without saying that I'll be glad to help it along."[62]

Mr. Piper contends that Fitzgerald "borrowed more directly from *Vandover and the Brute* than from any of Norris's other books" and that "this indebtedness is seen most strikingly in Fitzgerald's second novel *The Beautiful and Damned*, published in 1922, and in his short story 'May Day,' which at one time was a discarded beginning to this novel."[63] Certainly the following letter of August 26, 1920, to Harold Loeb evinces a partiality for *Vandover* and *McTeague*:

> I hope you didn't go to much trouble to locate *Blix*. I went to those stores you told me of & in the seventh one located it in the *25 cent* pile. What luck!
> But its [*sic*] no good—not to be compared with Vandover and McTeague. But, nevertheless, thanks a lot for looking it up and letting me know.[64]

In a 1921 review of another of Charles Norris's novels—*Brass*— he observed that by appealing "to the sense of smell or of hearing rather than by the commoner form of word painting" Frank Norris had achieved throughout *McTeague* an air of authenticity.[65] But perhaps the inscription on the flyleaf of Miss Graham's edition of *The Octopus* reveals most adequately his general and lasting respect for the work of Frank Norris:

> Sheilah from Scott
> Frank Norris after writing three great books died in 1902 at the age of just thirty. He was our most promising man and might have gone further than Drieser [*sic*] or the others. He claimed to be a disiple [*sic*] of Zola the naturalist, but in many ways he was better than Zola.
> The time of the events is about 1880

Fitzgerald had opinions on William Dean Howells, Stephen Crane, and Mark Twain too. He once cited Howells as a figure of the Victorian era in whom "a little boy could find little that was inspiring."[66] He thought very highly of *The Red Badge of Courage* and considered "the great central parts of 'Huckleberry Finn' " to constitute one of the "great English classics."[67] Mr. Piper commented in the *Fitzgerald Newsletter*:[68]

> F, like Hemingway and many another of that generation, was a lifelong admirer of the fiction of Mark Twain. His presentation copy of Van Wyck Brooks' *The Ordeal of Mark Twain* (1920), now among the other books of his library at Princeton, is underlined and annotated. And we find him writing Edmund Wilson in 1921 (CU, p. 256) that he has just finished reading Albert Bigelow Paine's three-volume biography of Mark Twain and thinks it "excellent." He was a member of the Mark Twain Society. And in 1935 when Cyril Clemens, president of this society, asked him

for a short tribute, F sent him the following statement about
Huckleberry Finn that is now published for the first time. It was
read aloud during the Mark Twain Society's banquet on Nov. 30,
1935, celebrating the centenary of his birth, and a copy is among
the F papers at Princeton.

"Huckleberry Finn took the first journey *back*. He was the first
to look *back* at the republic from the perspective of the West. His
eyes were the first eyes that ever looked at us objectively that
were not eyes from overseas. There were mountains at the frontier
but he wanted more than mountains to look at with his restless
eyes—he wanted to find out about men and how they lived together. And because he turned back we have him forever."[69]

Mr. Piper concluded his comments by saying that Mr. Clemens
described the banquet to him and then mentioned a visit to
Thomas Hardy in England in 1925 during which the novelist told
Clemens that "he had read and been greatly impressed by TSOP"
[*This Side of Paradise*], a book Fitzgerald once termed "a Romance and a Reading List"[70] and confessed in 1936 that "the
number of subheads I used . . . was one of the few consciously
original things" about it.[71] Although *Huckleberry Finn* may or
may not have influenced the composition of *This Side of Paradise*, the boy's story genre, a type of fiction Fitzgerald referred to
often while attending Princeton, certainly did—which brings us to
the twentieth century.

Reviewing for *The Nassau Literary Magazine* Booth Tarkington's *Penrod and Sam*, Scott Fitzgerald wrote:

> Mr. Tarkington has done what so many authors of juvenile books
> fail to do: he has admitted the unequaled snobbishness of boy-
> hood and has traced the neighborhood social system which, with
> Penrod and Sam at the top, makes possible more than half the
> stories. . . . Where Mr. Tarkington gets his knowledge of child
> psychology, I am unable to understand. It has become a tradition
> to mention Tom Brown as an ideal boy's story, but as a matter of
> fact, the heroes of Owen Johnston [*sic*], Compton McKenzie [*sic*],
> and Booth Tarkington are far more interesting and far truer to
> facts.[72]

In another review, this time of E. F. Benson's *David Blaize*, written for the same magazine in the same year (1917), Fitzgerald
observed:

Of late years there have been really good boys' stories, with the
boy treated from a subjective point of view neither cynically nor
sentimentally. In the class belong *The Varmint, Youth's Encounter, Seventeen,* and perhaps a new book, *David Blaize,* by
E. F. Benson, author of *Dodo.* . . . Mr. Benson's indebtedness to
Compton MacKenzie and Kipling is very great. Swinburne intro-
duces David to literature as he did Michael in *Youth's Encounter.* . . .[73]

In a letter of 1950 to Carlos Baker, Christian Gauss recalled "that
we one day fell into a discussion of Stevenson's advice to young
writers about playing the sedulous ape . . . Scott said that he had
imitated Joyce, (*The Portrait of the Author* [*sic*] *as a Young
Man*) and Compton McKenzie [*sic*], in parts of *This Side of
Paradise*"[74]; and in a letter of 1921 to Frances Newman, Fitzgerald
admitted that Mackenzie had been the major literary influence
on his first novel—an influence only a few of the critics had
detected:

> While it astonished me that so few critics mentioned the influ-
> ence of Sinister Street on This Side of Paradise, I feel sure that
> it was much more in intention than in literal fact. It occurred to
> me to write an American version of the history of that sort of
> young man—in which, no doubt, I was hindered by lack of perspec-
> tive as well as by congenital short-comings.
>
> But I was also hindered by a series of resemblances between
> my life and that of Michael Fane which, had I been a more
> conscientious man, might have precluded my ever attempting an
> autobiographical novel. I have five copies of Youth's Encounter
> at present in my library, sent me by people who stumbled on the
> book and thought that it was an amazing parallel to my own life.
> When I was twenty-one and began This Side of Paradise my
> literary taste was so unformed that Youth's Encounter was still
> my "perfect book." My book quite naturally shows the influence
> to a marked degree. However, I resent your details. . . .
> You seem to be unconscious that even MacKenzie had his
> sources such as Dorian Grey [*sic*] and None Other Gods and that
> occasionally we may have drunk at the same springs. . . . I sent
> the novel to Mencken with the confession that it derived itself
> from MacKenzie, Wells and Tarkington, with half a dozen addi-
> tional overtones, but there are comparisons you brought up that
> make me as angry as my book evidently made you.[75]

Fitzgerald's reference to Wells in this letter is of particular significance since, as has been frequently pointed out, Wells was the
second most important literary influence on *This Side of Paradise*.
James E. Miller (*The Fictional Technique of Scott Fitzgerald*,
pp. 14 and 15; see note 7) documents the author's early reaction
to the work of Wells:

> In 1917, he wrote to Edmund Wilson of a Wells novel: "I think
> that *The New Machiavelli* is the greatest English novel of the
> century" (*The Crack-Up*, p. 247). But Fitzgerald's interest in
> Wells was not confined to his novels. In another letter, he asked
> Wilson: "Have you read Well's [sic] *Boon, The Mind of the Race*,
> (Doran—1916) It's marvellous!" (*Ibid.*, p. 248). . . . In this same
> letter, Fitzgerald said, "I'm rather bored here [Princeton] but
> I . . . read Wells and Rousseau. I read Mrs. Gerould's *British
> Novelists Limited* and think she underestimates Wells but is right
> in putting McKenzie [sic] at the head of his school" (*Ibid.*). . . .
> In the early part of 1918, Fitzgerald wrote to Wilson: "In
> everything except my romantic Chestertonian orthodoxy I still
> agree with the early Wells on human nature and the 'no hope for
> Tono Bungay' theory" (*Ibid.*, p. 252). . . .
> But probably the most revealing evidence concerning the in-
> fluences on *This Side of Paradise* is in the book itself: "First,
> and partly by accident, they [Amory and his comrades] struck
> on certain books, a definite type of biographical novel that Amory
> christened quest books. In the quest book the hero set off in life
> armed with the best weapons and avowedly intending to use them
> as such weapons are usually used, to push their possessors ahead
> as selfishly and blindly as possible, but the heroes of the quest
> books discovered that there might be a more magnificent use for
> them. 'None Other Gods,' 'Sinister Street,' and 'The Research
> Magnificent' were examples of such books . . ." (131) [76]

The almost unparalleled increase of power from *This Side of
Paradise* (1920) and *The Beautiful and Damned* (1921-22) to *The
Great Gatsby* (1925) would be more inexplicable than it is if it
were not for our knowledge of Scott Fitzgerald's ability to discard
forces not conducive to bettering his fiction—in this case Mackenzie and Wells—and to take up new ones.

Shortly after finishing *The Beautiful and Damned*, the author
made a list of the ten most important novels for *The Chicago
Tribune*, calling *Nostromo* "the greatest novel since 'Vanity Fair'
(possibly excluding 'Madame Bovary')." [77] In 1922 he referred to

Conrad more than once, and in 1923, he described a passage from
Youth as "one of the most remarkable passages of English prose
written these thirty years."[78]

Conrad's theory that art should pursue the truth—"what is
enduring and essential"—had been set forth in the preface to
The Nigger of the "Narcissus." Fitzgerald wrote in his introduction to the 1934 Modern Library edition of *Gatsby*:

> Now that this book is being reissued, the author would like to
> say that never before did one try to keep his artistic conscience
> as pure as during the ten months put into doing it. Reading it
> over one can see how it could have been improved—yet without
> feeling guilty of any discrepancy from the truth, as far as I saw
> it; truth or rather the *equivalent* of the truth, the attempt at
> honesty of imagination. I had just re-read Conrad's preface to
> *The Nigger*, and I had recently been kidded half haywire by
> critics who felt that my material was such as to preclude all
> dealing with mature persons in a mature world.

That art should pursue the truth was not the only idea in the
preface that Scott Fitzgerald responded to. Conrad had gone on
to say:

> All art, therefore, appeals primarily to the senses. . . . And it is
> only through complete, unswerving devotion to the perfect blend-
> ing of form and substance; it is only through an unremitting
> never-discouraged care for the shape and ring of sentences that
> an approach can be made to plasticity, to colour; and the light of
> magic suggestiveness may be brought to play for an evanescent
> instant over the commonplace surface of words. . . .

Where there were verbosity and sloppiness in the earlier books,
there is, in *The Great Gatsby*, "care for the shape and ring of
sentences"; instead of the obvious word or phrase, there is "magic
suggestiveness"; whereas, previously, he had tended to be abstract,
Fitzgerald now works through the senses.[79] And finally, as almost
all of the critics observed, *Gatsby* was the first (perhaps the only)
Fitzgerald novel to show "the perfect blending of form and sub-
stance."

The author benefited from Conrad's techniques too. In 1949
John Jamieson wondered if "the conscious technical inspiration
of *The Great Gatsby*" had come from *Lord Jim*.[80] From external
and internal evidence, surely there should be no hesitation in

answering him affirmatively. During 1938 or 1939 Fitzgerald called *Lord Jim* "a great book,"[81] and many similarities are shared by his Nick and Conrad's Marlow. The device of the sympathetic, intelligent observer, which many critics have erroneously ascribed to the influence of James, was important for *The Last Tycoon* as well as for *Gatsby*:

> This love affair is the meat of the book—though I am going to treat it, remember, as it comes through to Cecilia. That is to say by making Cecilia, at the moment of her telling the story, an intelligent and observant woman, I shall grant myself the privilege, as Conrad did, of letting her imagine the actions of the characters. Thus, I hope to get the verisimilitude of a first person narrative, combined with a Godlike knowledge of all events that happen to my characters.[82]

Although *Tender Is the Night* does not use the observer, it shows the influence of two other Conrad techniques: "the dying fall" and "lingering after-effects." Fitzgerald remarked in a 1934 letter to John Peale Bishop that both he and Hemingway took "the dying fall"—which, in contrast to the dramatic ending, is a gradual letting down or tapering off—from Conrad. He told Bishop that this was valuable to him in *Tender* for the following reason: "I did not want to subject the reader to a series of nervous shocks because it was a novel that was inevitably close to whoever read it in my generation." He went on to explain to Bishop that there was no need to use "the dying fall" in *Gatsby*, however, since the persons treated, bootleggers and crooks, were not close to the feelings of most human beings.[83] In another 1934 letter—this one to Ernest Hemingway—he said that the "lingering after-effects" tried in *Tender* were also inspired by Joseph Conrad:

> The theory back of it I got from Conrad's preface to *The Nigger,* that the purpose of a work of fiction is to appeal to the lingering after-effects in the reader's mind as differing from, say, the purpose of oratory or philosophy which respectively leave people in a fighting or thoughtful mood.[84]

Scott Fitzgerald's new posture as (in Dean Gauss's words) "an earnest and competent student of the art of writing"[85] can be demonstrated best perhaps by examining his views on two American novelists—Hemingway, who, next to Conrad, was the most vital contemporary influence on his work, and Thomas Wolfe. Reporting on *In Our Time* during 1926,[86] Fitzgerald said:

> When I try to think of any contemporary American short stories as good as "Big Two-Hearted River," the last one in the book, only Gertrude Stein's "Melanctha," Anderson's "The Egg," and Lardner's "Golden Honeymoon" come to mind. It is the account of a boy on a fishing trip—he hikes, pitches his tent, cooks dinner, sleeps, and next morning casts for trout. Nothing more—but I read it with the most breathless unwilling interest I have experienced since Conrad first bent my reluctant eyes upon the sea.

He continued his remarks, stating that the stories make you "aware of something temperamentally new." This is Hemingway's ability to give his characters an emotion "without the aid of a comment or a pointing finger." The reader understands the meaning without much exposition; the dialogue tells everything. Of the construction, he noted, "There is no tail, no sudden change of pace at the end to throw into relief what has gone before." Hemingway cultivated a prose in which "there is not a bit to spare." Fitzgerald implied his own position when he said: "Material, however closely observed, is as elusive as the moment in which it has its existence unless it is purified by an incorruptible style and by the catharsis of a passionate emotion."

Scott Fitzgerald's admiration for Hemingway's work persisted throughout his life. In 1939 he called *A Farewell to Arms* one of the "great English classics"[87]; in 1940 he declared that *For Whom the Bell Tolls* was "a fine novel, better than anybody else writing could do" and in the same letter, said of *To Have and Have Not*: "There is observation and writing in that that the boys will be imitating with a vengeance—paragraphs and pages that are right up with Dostoiefski in their undeflected intensity."[88] Glenway Wescott maintained that Fitzgerald's esteem for Hemingway was so extreme that he felt he no longer had to write serious material, that Hemingway could be entrusted with this.[89] Wescott overstated the case. Still, Scott Fitzgerald did recognize the danger to his craft inherent in the enthusiasm he experienced over his friend's efforts. He said in 1934:

> I think it is obvious that my respect for your artistic life is absolutely unqualified, that save for a few of the dead or dying old men you are the only man writing fiction in America that I

look up to very much. There are pieces and paragraphs of your
work that I read over and over—in fact, I stopped myself doing
it for a year and a half because I was afraid that your particular
rhythms were going to creep in on mine by process of infiltration.
Perhaps you will recognize some of your remarks in *Tender*, but
I did every damn thing I could to avoid that.[90]

In the same letter, he told Hemingway that he had reinforced
Conrad's concept of lingering after-effects: ". . . you felt that the
true line of a work of fiction was to take a reader up to a high
emotional pitch but then let him down or ease him off. You gave
no aesthetic reason for this—nevertheless, you convinced me."
Hemingway clearly extended Fitzgerald's technical knowledge of
writing and symbolized to him that same high ideal of art that
he had found in Keats and Conrad. The author jotted down in
his notebooks: "Nevertheless value of Ernest's feeling about the
pure heart when writing—in other words the comparatively pure
heart, the 'house in order.' "[91]

The fact that Thomas Wolfe was neither a "shaper" nor a
"pruner," interested neither in form nor economy, was the basis
of Fitzgerald's view of his work. Wolfe poured himself out, marshaled his material in a "gawky and profuse way"[92] and as a result
was only "half-grown artistically."[93] In reply to Fitzgerald's advice
that he attempt to be a more conscious artist, Wolfe commented,
"a great writer is not only a leaver-outer but also a putter-inner,"
citing Shakespeare, Cervantes, and Dostoyevski as evidence.[94]
This did not lessen Fitzgerald's antagonism toward the sprawling
novel, an antagonism based on what was or was not communicated
as well as on style: ". . . his awful secret transpires at every crevice
—he did not have anything particular to say! The stuff about the
GREAT VITAL HEART OF AMERICA is just simply corny."
Wolfe had recapitulated Whitman, Dostoyevski, Nietzsche, and
Milton; "unlike Joyce and T. S. Eliot and Ernest Hemingway,"
he had "nothing really new to add." Why? Because he had failed
to find "a solid gold bar like Ernest's courage, or Josef Conrad's
art or D. H. Lawrence's intense cohabitations." Instead, he had
told us what we already knew, that everything was a "mess" and
that it was "too bad about the individual."[95] In his copy of *Of
Time and the River*, Fitzgerald wrote: "All this has been about as
good as Dodsworth for chapter after Chapter," and "Trite, trite,
trite, trite, page after page after page." Nevertheless, he had to

admit that with all his faults Wolfe had not committed "the cardinal sin" of composing a book that did not continue "to live."[96]

Of course, Scott Fitzgerald was affected by other contemporary authors and works. He said in 1940 that although Kafka would not have a "wide public," *The Trial* and *Amerika* were two novels that writers were "never able to forget,"[97] and that Mann's *Death in Venice* impressed him as "art, of the school of Flaubert—yet not derivative at all."[98] T. S. Eliot seemed "a very great person"[99]; Gertrude Stein would belong to the ages like "Booth and Seward."[100] He considered *Sister Carrie* to be "almost the first piece of American realism," a "damn good" achievement.[101] He admired the New Poetry movement, John Dos Passos' *Three Soldiers*, Sinclair Lewis' *Babbitt*, Thomas Boyd's *Through the Wheat*, Woodward Boyd's *Love Legend*, E. E. Cummings' *The Enormous Room*, Sherwood Anderson's *Many Marriages*, Marcel Proust's *Remembrance of Things Past*, Oswald Spengler's *The Decline of the West*, Edmund Wilson, Willa Cather, and Edith Wharton.[102] It must be remembered, too, that Scott Fitzgerald was very much a part of the literary milieu of the time as book dedications alone would indicate. He visited John Galsworthy, James Joyce, Edith Wharton, Compton Mackenzie, Gertrude Stein, Theodore Dreiser; he knew Edmund Wilson, John Peale Bishop, H. L. Mencken, Ring Lardner, John Dos Passos, Thomas Wolfe, Ernest Hemingway; he carried on sustained correspondence with between seventy-five and one hundred noteworthy men and women.

Fitzgerald's reading though fairly wide was quite selective. He picked the periods, the artists, and the genres that were necessary to his own particular genius—the lyric poetry of the English Renaissance (Shakespeare), the early nineteenth century (romantic poets, especially Keats), the late nineteenth century (French symbolists, Browning, Swinburne, Kipling), the twentieth century (Brooke, Eliot); the novel of social realism (Thackeray, Butler, Norris, Dreiser, Proust, Wharton); the "novel of selection" (Flaubert, James, Joyce, Conrad, Cather, Hemingway). When he outgrew certain authors, for example Wilde, Wells, and Mackenzie, he found new, more helpful models. As Professor Trilling contended, "It is hard to overestimate the benefit which came to Fitzgerald from his having consciously placed himself in the line of the great." Surely, he took thought, "which, for a writer, means really knowing what his predecessors have done." Surely, he had "intellectual courage," a "grasp . . . of the traditional resources available to him," a "connection with tradition and with mind."[103]

NOTES

1 *F. Scott Fitzgerald: The Man and His Work,* ed. Alfred Kazin, Cleveland [1951], p. 77.

2 *Ibid.,* p. 179.

3 *The Far Side of Paradise,* Boston [1951], p. 103.

4 *The Stories of F. Scott Fitzgerald,* ed. Malcolm Cowley, New York, 1951, p. xvi.

5 *The Crack-Up,* ed. Edmund Wilson [New York, 1945], p. 329.

6 Kazin, p. 201.

7 My *main* concern has not been to trace specific literary influences on Fitzgerald's work. For two essays and one book which do this effectively, I refer the reader to Robert Wooster Stallman, "Conrad and *The Great Gatsby,*" *Twentieth Century Literature,* I, No. 1 (Apr., 1955), 5-12; Henry Dan Piper, "Frank Norris and Scott Fitzgerald," *The Huntington Library Quarterly,* XIX, No. 4 (Aug., 1956), 393-400; and James E. Miller, *The Fictional Technique of Scott Fitzgerald,* The Hague, 1957. My sources include Fitzgerald's published canon, his notebooks, his letters, the volumes he gave to Miss Sheilah Graham during the late '30's (about 200), and the volumes he owned (about 1,000). Let me describe the fate of these last. Shortly after the author's death in 1940, the books in his library were deposited in the Princeton University Library. Subsequently, many of them were returned to Mrs. Samuel J. Lanahan, his daughter. Alexander D. Wainwright, Assistant Chief of the Department of Rare Books and Special Collections, compiled two lists—one the books from Fitzgerald's library remaining in the Rare Book Department at Princeton and the other the books returned to Mrs. Lanahan. These lists appear in my dissertation, *Scott Fitzgerald: Romantic and Realist,* which is deposited in the Columbia University Library. A third list of Fitzgerald's books that had no markings or signs of ownership was compiled by another member of the Princeton Library staff. This list was designated "Miscellaneous" and the books tabulated were dispersed. Since the works on the "Miscellaneous" list are largely nonsignificant, I feel it necessary to mention only those of particular interest: *Anthologie des Poètes Français Contemporains* (Nouvelle édition, 1866-1926); Butler, *The Authoress of the Odyssey;* Conrad, *Chance, Lord Jim, Nostromo, A Personal Record, The Rescue, The Rover, A Set of Six, Youth and Two Other Stories;* Keats, *The Complete Poetical Works and Letters* (Cambridge

edition), Colvin's *Life*; Thackeray, *The History of Henry Esmond, Esq.* Additional authors who should be mentioned: Blake, Browning, Carlyle, Flaubert, Homer, Kipling, Laforgue, Masefield, Poe, Proust, Shaw, Wells, Wharton, Wilde, Valéry. I would like also to point out to the reader that my discussion of Fitzgerald's library is, for the most part, limited to his acquaintance with literature, and even here I have been selective. Finally, to conclude a long note, allow me to express sincere thanks to Mrs. Lanahan and Miss Graham for making available unpublished materials.

8 Occasionally in the margins of the books he purchased for Miss Graham, Fitzgerald translated Latin words and phrases.

9 Fitzgerald's scholastic record at both Newman and Princeton is on his Princeton transcript, which is in the Office of the Registrar, Princeton University. Probably because the Newman record is on the back of the Princeton record, it has not previously been noted.

10 That Fitzgerald provided Miss Graham with J. B. Bury's *A History of Greece* and *Outline for Review: Greek History* by C. B. Newton and E. B. Treat indicates, perhaps, at least as much interest on his part in Greek civilization as in Greek literature. The inscription on the Newton-Treat volume (which forms part of the materials Miss Graham recently donated to the Princeton Library) reads: "For S. G. For her proficiency in pre-Socratic philosophy, Hellenistic anthropology and Trojan archeology from Her Loving Prof T. Themestocles Smith Olymic [sic] games, 1910." The Bury volume, along with the other books Fitzgerald gave her, is located in Miss Graham's personal library at Westport, Connecticut.

11 Fitzgerald to Frances Scott Fitzgerald, June 7, 1940, F. Scott Fitzgerald Papers, Princeton University Library.

12 *The Nassau Literary Magazine,* LXXII, No. 3 (June, 1916), [137].

13 Fitzgerald to Frances Scott Fitzgerald, November 15, 1938, Fitzgerald Papers.

14 Fitzgerald's outline for Miss Graham's reading in this work is quite specific and elaborate. He remarked, regarding the Fifth Story of the Fourth Day: ". . . inspiration of Keat's [sic] 'Pot of Basil.' "

15 The "Literary" section of the notebooks, Fitzgerald Papers.

16 Review of *Verses in Peace and War,* by Shane Leslie, *The Nassau Literary Magazine,* LXXIII, No. 3 (June, 1917), 153.

17 Sonnets 29, 30, 57, 94, and 116. Songs: "Blow, blow, thou winter wind"; "Come away, come away, Death"; "Crabbed age and youth"; "Fear no more the heat o' the sun"; "Full fathom five thy father lies"; "It was a lover and his lass"; "O Mistress mine! where are you roaming?"; "On a day, alack the day!"; "Take, O take those lips away"; "Tell me where is fancy bred"; "Under the greenwood tree"; and

"When icicles hang by the wall." The lines "Love's not Time's fool, though rosy lips and cheeks / Within his bending sickle's compass come" in Sonnet 116 are bracketed.

18 Fitzgerald to Frances Scott Fitzgerald, November 11, 1938, Fitzgerald Papers.

19 *Ibid.*, March 11, 1939.

20 Of *The Decline and Fall,* Fitzgerald said in the copy he bought for Miss Graham: "It is important to remember that Gibbon wrote this history in the late 18th century (1765-1785) *before* the French Revolution and the Industrial Revolution when men believed that the 'Age of Reason' had indeed arrived. Yet the stuff is full of irony—especially when he speaks of the church and compares the rich men of antiquity to those of his time—to the pretended *advantage* of the latter."

21 Besides the authors and works I discuss under the early nineteenth century, Fitzgerald probably read: Cooper (*The Last of the Mohicans*); Irving; Balzac (*La Cousine Bette; Eugénie Grandet; Droll Stories; Père Goriot; La Peau de Chagrin; César Birotteau*); Goethe (*Faust; The Sorrows of Werther*); Hugo (*Notre-Dame de Paris*); De Musset; Rousseau; Stendahl (*La Chartreuse de Parme; Le Rouge et le Noir*). The reader will have noticed that my listings according to literary periods are necessarily somewhat arbitrary.

22 "To Night"; "O world! O life!"; "Stanzas written in Dejection"; "One word is too often"; "To a Skylark"; "To the Moon"; "When the lamp is shattered"; "I met a traveller"; "Ode to the West Wind"; "Lines written among the Euganean Hills"; "I arise from dreams"; "Ariel to Miranda"; "The fountains mingle"; and "Music, when soft voices." Those who have perused *The Crack-Up* and *Beloved Infidel* are aware of Fitzgerald's practice of sending study lists to both his daughter and Miss Graham. The latter has informed me that he was seriously considering writing a book on education before his death.

23 We are told in an undated letter to Mrs. Mary Fitzgerald (Fitzgerald Papers) that "The Prisoner of Chillon" was perhaps the first poem Scott Fitzgerald ever heard:

Tell father I visited the
"—seven pillars of Gothic mould
in Chillon's dungeons deep and old,"
& thought of the first poem I ever heard, or was [it] "The Raven."

In addition to the works cited, he probably read *Manfred* and Maurois' *Life of Byron.*

24 The chapters very likely refer to H. Nicolson's *Byron: The Last Journey.*

25 "On First Looking into Chapman's Homer"; "Isabella"; "The Eve of St. Agnes"; "Ode to a Nightingale"; "Fancy"; "Bards of Passion and of Mirth"; "Ode on Melancholy"; "When I Have Fears"; "Frag-

ment of an Ode to Maia"; "In Drear-Nighted December"; "The Eve of St. Mark"; and "Bright Star." Besides some of these, he also marked "To Autumn" in Palgrave's *The Golden Treasury*.

26 Unaddressed, undated letter, Fitzgerald Papers.

27 Fitzgerald to Morton [———], August 9, 1939, Fitzgerald Papers. Miss Graham's enrollment in Fitzgerald's "College of One" was occasioned by his reciting "Ode on a Grecian Urn" (*Beloved Infidel*, New York [1958], p. 259). He inscribed a copy of *The Beautiful and Damned* for her in this way: "To the Beautiful from the almost damned./'What struggle to escape.'/With love from/Scott Fitzgerald/to Sheilah Graham/New Years 1940." That he could joke about his most cherished poem ("Grecian Urn") both early and late is evidenced by "To My Unused Greek Book" (1916) and the following quotation taken from a blank page at the back of Palgrave's *The Golden Treasury* (Miss Graham's library): "'S' as good as new! And think how long it was buried. We could learn a lot of history from it—about the rubes in ancient history, more than from any poetry about them. Those pictures on it must tell a story about their Gods, maybe, or just ordinary people—something about life in the sticks at a place called Tempe. Or maybe it was in the Arcady Valley. These guys chasing the dames are either gods or just ordinary people—it doesn't give names on the cup. They are sure tearing after them and the dames are trying to get away. Look—this guys [*sic*] got a flute, or maybe its [*sic*] an obo [*sic*] and they're going to town. etc. etc."

28 Fitzgerald to Frances Scott Fitzgerald, July 29, 1940, Fitzgerald Papers.

29 New York, 1920, p. 93.

30 New York, 1922, p. 8.

31 Fitzgerald to Frances Scott Fitzgerald, August 3, 1940, Fitzgerald Papers.

32 His own library contained copies of Laforgue's *Oeuvres*, Rimbaud's *Oeuvres*, and Verlaine's *Choix de Poésies*, while Rimbaud's *Une Saison en Enfer* and *Poésies* as well as Verlaine's *Les Plus Belles Pages* are with the volumes he bought for Miss Graham. The Rimbaud poems he found most congenial were "Le Dormeur du Val," "Bateau Ivre," "Les Etrennes des Orphelins," "Les Assis," "Voyelles"; and among Verlaine's, "Melancholia," "Fêtes Galantes," "Clair de Lune," "Romances sans Paroles," "Il pleure dans mon coeur," "Sagesse," "Jadis et Naguère," "Paysages Tristes," "Chanson d'Automne," "Aquarelles." Fitzgerald received B in French A and E in French B at Newman and at Princeton 5 in French 203, 4 in French 204, 5 in French 301, 4 in French 302, 2 in French 401, and 3 in French 402.

33 Other late nineteenth-century French and European authors and works Fitzgerald probably read: Chekhov (*The Cherry Orchard and Other Plays; Letters on the Short Story, the Drama and Other Literary*

Topics; Uncle Vanya); Dostoyevsky (*Crime and Punishment; The Brothers Karamazov; The Insulted and Injured; The Possessed;* E. J. Simmons' *Dostoevski, The Making of a Novelist*); Flaubert (*Three Tales; L'Education Sentimentale;* Francis Steegmüller's *Flaubert and Madame Bovary*); France (*The Revolt of the Angels; The Red Lily*); Gautier; Gogol (*The Government Inspector and Other Plays*); Hegel; Huysmans (*A Rebours*); Ibsen (*Plays; A Doll's House*); Leblanc (*Arsène Lupin*); Louÿs (*Aphrodite*); Marx (*Capital; The Poverty of Philosophy; Manifesto of the Communist Party*); Maupassant (*The Complete Short Stories*); Nietzsche (*The Genealogy of Morals*); Renan (*The Life of Jesus*); Schopenhauer (*Studies in Pessimism*); Sudermann (*The Song of Songs*); Tolstoi (*War and Peace; Anna Karenina; Master and Man, The Kreutzer Sonata, Dramas*); Turgenev (*Smoke*) Zola.

34 John Jamieson to Arthur Mizener, April, 1949, Princeton University Library.

35 Fitzgerald to Jamieson, April 7, 1934, Princeton University Library.

36 Fitzgerald to Bishop, April 7, 1934, Fitzgerald Papers.

37 Page 423.

38 Wilson, p. 308. Besides the books already named, Fitzgerald had copies of Thackeray's *The Virginians* and *The Rose and the Ring.*

39 Mizener, p. 89.

40 A note in Fitzgerald's copy of Butler's *Note-Books,* Mrs. Samuel J. Lanahan.

41 "One Hundred False Starts," *The Saturday Evening Post,* CCV, No. 36 (Mar. 4, 1933), 13. Besides the *Note-Books,* the author either owned, or purchased for Miss Graham, Butler's *Erewhon* and *Erewhon Revisited; The Way of All Flesh; Life and Habit; Alps and Sanctuaries of Piedmont and the Canton Ticino.*

42 Writers and works of the Victorian period in England that Fitzgerald probably read and are not mentioned in the discussion: Arnold (*Poetical Works*); J. M. Barrie; Bennett (*The Old Wives' Tale; Accident; The Pretty Lady*); E. Brontë (*Wuthering Heights*); E. B. Browning (*Sonnets from the Portuguese*); Carlyle (*Heroes and Hero-Worship**); Carroll (*Through the Looking-Glass*); Darwin (*Origin of Species*); Dickens (*Hard Times; Barnaby Rudge; Great Expectations; The Old Curiosity Shop; The Pickwick Papers; David Copperfield; Reprinted Pieces; A Tale of Two Cities; Sketches by Boz; Nicholas Nickleby; Martin Chuzzlewit*); Dowson ("Cynara"; *Poems and Prose*); Fitzgerald (*Rubáiyát*); Hardy (*Tess of the D'Urbervilles*); Housman (*A Shropshire Lad*); Kipling ("The Drums of the Fore and Aft"**; *Life's Handicap; Soldiers Three; The Story of the Gadsbys; In Black and White; Plain Tales from the Hills; The Jungle Book; Depart-*

mental Ditties and Ballads and Barrack Room Ballads; "Gunga Din"); Meredith (*The Ordeal of Richard Feverel*); G. Moore (*Memoirs of My Dead Life; Esther Waters*); Newman; Pater; Pinero; D. G. Rossetti ("The Blessed Damozel"); Shaw (*Androcles and the Lion, Overruled, Pygmalion; Plays: Pleasant and Unpleasant*, Vols. I and II; *Man and Superman; Misalliance, The Dark Lady of the Sonnets, and Fanny's First Play; Heartbreak House; Nine Plays*); Spencer; Stevenson (*A Child's Garden of Verses; Learning to Write; New Arabian Nights; The Silverado Squatters*); Swinburne (*The Works; Poems*); Tennyson (*The Poetical Works*); Wilde (*Salomé, La Sainte Courtisane; Poems; The Ballad of Reading Gaol; Lady Windermere's Fan; An Ideal Husband; A Woman of No Importance; Salomé and Other Plays; The Harlot's House; The Happy Prince*).

* In "The Spire and the Gargoyle" (*The Nassau Literary Magazine*, LXXII, No. 7 [Feb., 1917]), Fitzgerald wrote: "Freshman year Carlisle's [*sic*] 'Heroes and Hero-Worship,' in the hands of an impassioned young instructor had interested him particularly . . . his philosophy of life was molded of two elements . . . the other, the three or four big ideas which he found in the plain speaking Scotchman, Carlyle."

** In a letter to Morton [———], August 9, 1939 (Fitzgerald Papers), Fitzgerald called this work one of the "great English classics."

43 Quotation from Wilson, p. 304. Works checked in *Poems and Plays* of Robert Browning: "My Last Duchess"; "Porphyria's Lover"; "The Pied Piper of Hamelin"; "The Lost Leader"; "Home-Thoughts, From Abroad"; "Home-Thoughts, From the Sea"; "The Laboratory"; "Love among the Ruins"; "Life in a Love"; "The Last Ride Together"; "Youth and Art."

44 Miss Graham's copy of Swinburne's *Poems*.

45 Fitzgerald to Miss Frances Turnbull, November 9, 1938, Fitzgerald Papers.

46 Both letters in the Fitzgerald Papers. That Fitzgerald purchased a number of Wilde's plays for Miss Graham as well as works by H. G. Wells, Compton Mackenzie, etc., indicates that although he might repudiate an early influence, he could never utterly abandon an author he once liked.

47 Review of *Many Marriages*, by Sherwood Anderson, *New York Herald*, Mar. 4, 1923, Sec. 9, p. 5.

48 Kazin, p. 144.

49 Wilson, p. 310.

50 Mizener, p. 170.

51 Fitzgerald to Morton [———], August 9, 1939, Fitzgerald Papers.

52 "The Romance of Money," *Three Novels of F. Scott Fitzgerald*, New York [1953], pp. xviii-xix.

53 Wilson, p. 288.

54 Fitzgerald to Mrs. Bayard Turnbull, September 10, 1932, Princeton University Library.

55 "How to Waste Material," *The Bookman*, LXIII, No. 3 (May, 1926), 262. His own library contained copies of *The Pilgrimage of Henry James* (by Van Wyck Brooks) and *The Art of the Novel* and he gave to Miss Graham: *The Portrait of a Lady; The Bostonians; Washington Square; Roderick Hudson; The Europeans*; and *The Aspern Papers, Louisa Pallant, The Modern Warning*.

56 Fitzgerald to Alida Bigelow (later Mrs. Francis D. Butler), September 22, 1919, Princeton University Library.

57 Review of *Brass*, by Charles Norris, *The Bookman*, LIV, No. 3 (Nov., 1921), 253.

58 Page 224. The passage was composed during the summer of 1919. In a review of *Prejudices: Second Series* (*The Bookman*, LIII, No. 1 [Mar., 1921]), Fitzgerald said that Mencken had "done more for the national letters than any man alive." In "How to Waste Material" (see note 55), he said Mencken had "always been ethical rather than aesthetic" and so had "begotten a family of hammer and tongs men—insensitive, suspicious of glamour, preoccupied exclusively with the external, the contemptible, the 'national' and the drab." And in his introduction to the Modern Library edition of *The Great Gatsby*, New York [1934], he wrote: ". . . the world of imagination" was "the world that Mencken made stable in the days when he was watching over us." Fitzgerald owned *Prejudices: First Series; Prejudices: Second Series; Prejudices: Third Series; Prejudices: Fourth Series; The Philosophy of Friedrich Nietzsche; A Book of Burlesques; Heliogabalus, A Buffoonery in Three Acts* (with G. J. Nathan); *In Defense of Women; Treatise on Right and Wrong; Treatise on the Gods; A Book of Prefaces*; and *Menckeniana, A Schimpflexikon*.

59 See note 7.

60 Pages 396-397.

61 Fitzgerald Papers.

62 Mencken to Fitzgerald, October 7 [no year], Fitzgerald Papers.

63 "Frank Norris and Scott Fitzgerald," p. 393.

64 Harold Loeb Papers, Princeton University Library.

65 See note 57.

66 "Wait till You Have Children of Your Own!" *Woman's Home Companion*, LI (July, 1924), 13, 105.

67 Fitzgerald to Morton [——], August 9, 1939, Fitzgerald Papers.

68 No. 8 (Winter, 1960).

69 Authors and works of the late nineteenth century in the United States that Fitzgerald probably read and are not mentioned in the discussion: Alger (half a dozen volumes, including *Bound to Rise*); Bierce (*In the Midst of Life*); Clemens (*The Man That Corrupted*

Hadleyburg, and Other Stories and Essays; The Mysterious Stranger; Sketches New and Old; The Prince and the Pauper; What is Man? and Other Essays); Dana (*Two Years before the Mast*); R. H. Davis; J. Fox, Jr.; Howells (*Venetian Life*); W. James (*The Philosophy of William James*); London (*The Call of the Wild*); Longfellow (*Evangeline*); Poe* (*The Fall of the House of Usher*; "Ulalume"; "The Raven"; "The Bells"); J. W. Riley; Thoreau; Whitman (*Leaves of Grass*; "Pioneers, O Pioneers").

* See note 23. Fitzgerald said in Wilson (*The Crack-Up*), p. 174: "Father passed on to me certain ineradicable tastes in poetry: *The Raven* and *The Bells, The Prisoner of Chillon*." Poe probably influenced the language and tone of early stories like "The Mystery of the Raymond Mortgage" (1909) and "The Room with the Green Blinds" (1911).

70 The "Literary" section of the notebooks, Fitzgerald Papers.

71 Fitzgerald to Bennett Cerf, August 13, 1936, Fitzgerald Papers.

72 LXXII, No. 6 (Jan., 1917), [291]-292. Tipped in a copy of the Chatto & Windus (London) edition of *The Great Gatsby* in the Princeton University Library is a letter from Fitzgerald to Julian Street, the first part of which reads: "My best to you! My contempt for Tarkington extends only to his character of being ashamed of his early sins & thus cutting out of his experience about ½ of life. He woke up one morning sober & 40, and thought that no one had ever been lascivious or drunk or vain except himself, & turned deliberately back to the illusions of his boyhood." (Probable date: 1928.)

73 LXXII, No. 7 (Feb., 1917), 343-344.

74 Private correspondence of Professor Carlos Baker, Department of English, Princeton University. In *The Fictional Technique of Scott Fitzgerald* (see note 7), p. 29, James E. Miller cites the following statement of Oscar Cargill (*Intellectual America: Ideas on the March*, New York, 1941, p. 349): "One might not suspect this [i.e. *A Portrait of the Artist* as model] from reading *This Side of Paradise*, which seems more of a travesty than a serious effort, yet such is the case." Miller then comments: "There is indication in *This Side of Paradise* that Fitzgerald had read Joyce's novel. He says at one point of Amory (*This Side of Paradise*, p. 224): 'He was puzzled and depressed by "A Portrait of the Artist as a Young Man" . . .' And there are certain lines of action in the two books which are similar: the detailed account of unhappy school life, the growing interest in literature, and the rejection of religion—in both cases, Catholicism. There is even an echo of Joyce's famous phrase (*A Portrait of the Artist as a Young Man* ['The Modern Library'; New York: Random House, 1928], p. 299), '. . . to forge in the smithy of my soul the uncreated conscience of my race,' in Fitzgerald's novel. Amory tells Tom D'Invilliers (*This Side of Paradise*, p. 230) that he 'represent[s] the critical conscious-

ness of the race,' and he refers to himself, near the end of the book
(p. 285), as 'preserved to help in building up the living consciousness
of the race.' The phrases are different, of course, but there is enough
similarity to suggest unconscious borrowing. However, there is no indication that Fitzgerald was consciously imitating Joyce's book; *A Portrait* was too much a novel of selection for Fitzgerald's taste at the
time. He was, like Amory, probably 'puzzled' by it." On pp. 34-35 of
his book, Miller asserts: "Mr. Cargill, in *Intellectual America* (p. 349),
stated that Fitzgerald's method of 'writing . . . dialogue as in a drama'
was 'suggested by the work of Joyce.' This is unlikely, for Fitzgerald
first used the method in 'The Debutante,' published in *The Smart Set*
in September, 1919, and later incorporated in *This Side of Paradise*
(pp. 179 ff.). *Ulysses,* in which Joyce first used the method, was
published as a book in 1922. Although it was serialized before 1922, it
seems improbable that Fitzgerald had seen it before then, especially
in view of his statement in a letter to Edmund Wilson dated June 29
[June 25?], 1922 (*The Crack-Up,* p. 26 [p. 260?]): 'I have Ullysses
[*sic*] from the Brick Row Bookshop & am starting it.' This statement
implies that Fitzgerald had not seen Joyce's novel before. Probably
the method is a carry-over for Fitzgerald from the writing of dialogue
and lyrics for musical comedies at Princeton." Fitzgerald possessed
copies of *Dubliners* (in which he checked "Two Gallants," "Counter-
parts," "The Dead," and wrote: "I am interested in the individual
only in his rel [relation] to society. We have wondered [*sic*] in
imaginary lonliness [*sic*] through imaginary woods for a hundred
years"), *Chamber Music, Pomes Penyeach, Ulysses* (in which there
is a card from Joyce dated 11.7.928), *A Portrait of the Artist as a
Young Man* (in which Joyce has inscribed on the front flyleaf: "To
Scott Fitzgerald/James Joyce/Paris/11.7.928"). On August 9, 1939,
he called *Dubliners* one of the "great English classics" (Fitzgerald to
Morton [——], Fitzgerald Papers), and on June 25, 1922, he said of
Ulysses: "I wish it was layed [*sic*] in America—there is something
about middle-class Ireland that depresses me inordinately—I mean
gives me a sort of hollow, cheerless pain. Half of my ancestors came
from just such an Irish strata or perhaps a lower one. The book makes
me feel appallingly naked" (Wilson, p. 260). He jotted in the "Literary" section of the notebooks: "Must listen for conversation style a la
Joyce" (Fitzgerald Papers), borrowed the term he used to describe
Dick Diver of *Tender Is the Night*—"a spoiled priest"—from *Ulysses*
(New York, 1934, p. 512), and at a 1928 dinner sketched a picture of
himself kneeling before Joyce, whose head is crowned with a halo
(Sylvia Beach, *Les Ecrivains Américains à Paris et Leurs Amis, 1920-
1930* [Paris, 1959], opposite p. 81).

75 *Frances Newman's Letters,* New York, 1929, pp. 40-42. For a detailed comparison between *This Side of Paradise* and *Sinister Street,*
the reader should consult Frederick J. Hoffman, *The Twenties,* New

York, 1955, pp. 100-103. Fitzgerald's interest in boys' stories affected not only the writing of his first novel, but also the Basil pieces of 1928. In fact, Basil tells us that he "had lived with such intensity on so many stories of boarding-school life" ("The Freshest Boy," *Taps at Reveille,* New York, 1935, p. 27).

76 Fitzgerald secured for Miss Graham Wells's *The Outline of History* and *Experiment in Autobiography* and Mackenzie's *Youth's Encounter* and *Sinister Street.* See note 46.

77 Mizener, p. 336. Conrad's name is mentioned on p. 233 of *This Side of Paradise.* For a comprehensive and convincing analysis of Fitzgerald's shift from "the novel of saturation" (Mackenzie, Wells, R. H. Benson) to "the novel of selection" (James, Wharton, Conrad, Cather, and Joyce), the reader should consult Miller's book. For Conrad's influence on *The Great Gatsby,* he should see R. W. Stallman's "Conrad and *The Great Gatsby*" (note 7), which states, among other valuable insights, "What he learned from Conrad includes not only the device of the perplexed narrator and turns of phrasing, but also themes and plot-situations, ambivalence of symbolism, etc.—in fact, the craft of the novel" (p. 5).

78 Review of *Through the Wheat,* by Thomas Boyd, *New York Evening Post,* May 26, 1923, Sec. 3, p. 715.

79 In 1933 Fitzgerald wrote that Conrad had defined "the serious business" of his profession "more clearly, more vividly than any man of our time": "My task is by the power of the written word to make you hear, to make you feel—it is, before all, to make you see" ("One Hundred False Starts"; see note 41).

80 Jamieson to Mizener, April, 1949, Princeton University Library.

81 Wilson, p. 288.

82 *The Last Tycoon, Three Novels of F. Scott Fitzgerald* (see note 52), pp. 139-140.

83 Fitzgerald to Bishop, April 7, 1934, Fitzgerald Papers.

84 Fitzgerald to Hemingway, June 1, 1934, Fitzgerald Papers.

85 Letter of 1950 to Carlos Baker (see note 74). This is the sentence from which the quotation was taken: "To a much greater degree than Arthur Mizener or most critics realize, Scott too was and remained an earnest and competent student of the art of writing and this was one of the bonds between them" [Fitzgerald and Hemingway].

86 "How to Waste Material" (see note 55), pp. 264-265. The first reference Fitzgerald made to Hemingway appears in a letter he wrote to Perkins during 1924: "This is to tell you about a young man named Ernest Hemingway, who lives in Paris . . . writes for the *Transatlantic Review* & has a brillant future. I'd look him up right away. He's the real thing" (quoted by R. Burlingame, *Of Making Many Books,* New York, 1946, p. 47). The first letter of their correspondence, which extends over the period 1925-1935, is dated by Hemingway July 1, 1925.

87 Fitzgerald to Morton [——], August 9, 1939, Fitzgerald Papers.

88 Fitzgerald to Hemingway, November 8, 1940, Fitzgerald Papers.

89 Wilson, p. 325.

90 Fitzgerald to Hemingway, June 1, 1934, Fitzgerald Papers.

91 The "Literary" section of the notebooks, Fitzgerald Papers. An analysis of Hemingway's specific influence on Fitzgerald, comparable to Piper's work with Norris, Stallman's with Conrad, Hoffman's with Mackenzie, and Miller's with the shift from the "novel of saturation" to the "novel of selection," is needed. Because my purpose has been to explore the author's reading, and also because of space limitations, I have tried to be only suggestive regarding literary influences.

92 Fitzgerald to Mrs. Bayard Turnbull, March 15, 1935, Princeton University Library.

93 The "Literary" section of the notebooks, Fitzgerald Papers.

94 Wilson, p. 314.

95 Fitzgerald to Frances Scott Fitzgerald, November 29, 1940, Fitzgerald Papers.

96 *Ibid.*

97 Fitzgerald to Perkins, December 13, 1940, Fitzgerald Papers.

98 Fitzgerald to Frances Scott Fitzgerald, October 5, 1940, Fitzgerald Papers.

99 Fitzgerald to Mrs. Bayard Turnbull [June, 1933], Princeton University Library.

100 *Ibid.* [September, 1933], Princeton University Library.

101 Wilson, p. 288. See references above to Dreiser on pp. 67 and 69. Andrew Turnbull, Fitzgerald's new biographer, recently sent me the following quotation from a letter Fitzgerald wrote to Perkins (February 22, 1922): "I found that thing by Anatole France very interesting. It's the same thing that Mencken says about Hardy & Conrad & Dreiser, the thing that lives [lifts] them above the 'cerebral' novelists like Wells—the profound gesture of pity." Miss Graham says in *Beloved Infidel* that Fitzgerald thought of Dreiser as "his greatest contemporary."

I am also grateful to Mr. Turnbull for sending the following lists copied from Fitzgerald's Scrapbook III:

THE TEN BOOKS I HAVE ENJOYED MOST [CA. AUTUMN, 1922]:

1. Samuel Butler's "Notebooks." The mind and heart of my favorite Victorian.

2. "The Philosophy of Frederick Nietzsche" (H. L. Mencken). A keen hard intelligence interpreting the Great Modern Philosopher.

3. "Portrait of the Artist as a Young Man" (James Joyce). Because James Joyce is to be the most profound literary influence of the next fifty years.

4. "Zuleika Dobson" (Max Beerbohm). For the sheer delight of its exquisite snobbery.
5. "The Mysterious Stranger" (Mark Twain). Mark Twain in his most sincere mood. A book and a startling revelation.
6. "Nostromo" (Joseph Conrad). The great novel of the past fifty years, as Ulysses is the great novel of the future.
7. "Vanity Fair" (Thackeray). No explanation required.
8. "The Oxford Book of English Verse." This seems to me a better collection than Palgraves.
9. "Thais" (Anatole France). The great book of a man who is Wells and Shaw together.
10. "Seventeen" (Tarkington). The funniest book I've ever read.

SCOTT FITZGERALD LAYS SUCCESS TO READING [CA. WINTER, 1927]:

at 14. "The Varmint," Owen Johnson
at 16. "The Lord of the World," Robert Hugh Benson
at 18. "The Picture of Dorian Gray," Oscar Wilde
at 20. "Sinister Street," Compton MacKenzie
at 22. "Tono Bungay," H. G. Wells
at 24. "The Genealogy of Morals," Nietzsche
at 26. "The Brothers Karamazov"
at 28. Ludendorf's "Memoirs"
at 30. Spengler's "Decline of the West"

102 An analysis of the Fitzgerald-Wilson relationship has never been made and would no doubt prove extremely valuable. Miller (*The Fictional Technique of Scott Fitzgerald*) discusses Willa Cather's influence as does Stallman ("Conrad and *The Great Gatsby*") Oswald Spengler's. Twentieth-century writers and works that Fitzgerald probably read but are not mentioned in either the text or notes: Aiken; Anderson (*Winesburg, Ohio*); Beerbohm (*Seven Men; The Happy Hypocrite; A Christmas Garland; Yet Again; More; The Works*); S. V. Benét (*The Beginning of Wisdom*); R. H. Benson (*The Coward; The Religion of the Plain Man; Richard Raynal*); Bergson; J. P. Bishop (*Green Fruit; The Undertaker's Garland; Act of Darkness*); Bodenheim; E. Boyd (*Ireland's Literary Renaissance; Portraits: Real and Imaginary; Appreciations and Depreciations*); Brooke (*The Collected Poems; 1914 and Other Poems*; "The Soldier"); V. W. Brooks (*The Flowering of New England*); H. Broun (*Pieces of Hate and Other Enthusiasms*); Cabell (*The Cords of Vanity; Jurgen; Beyond Life; Figures of Earth*); Caldwell; Cather (*Death Comes for the Archbishop*); Chesterton (*The Man Who Was Thursday*); Conrad (*The Rover; Victory; Notes on Life and Letters; Notes on My Books; The Mirror of the Sea; The Secret Agent; Under Western Eyes; Almayer's*

Folly); Coward; Cummings (*Tulips and Chimneys*); Dos Passos (*A Pushcart at the Curb*); Dreiser (*The Titan; The Financier; The Color of a Great City; A Traveler at Forty; An American Tragedy*); Eliot (*Ash-Wednesday; For Lancelot Andrewes; Poems; The Waste Land*; "Portrait of a Lady"); Ellis; Faulkner (*Light in August; The Sound and the Fury; Sanctuary*); Ferber; Frost (*North of Boston*); H. B. Fuller; Gale; Galsworthy (*Another Sheaf; The White Monkey*); Garland; D. Garnett (*Lady into Fox*); Glasgow; Gide; Gorky (*Days with Lenin*); Hemingway (*Death in the Afternoon; The Sun also Rises; Men without Women; Three Stories & Ten Poems; Winner Take Nothing; The Torrents of Spring*); Hergesheimer (*Cytherea*); R. Herrick; S. Howard (*Three Flights Up*); E. W. Howe; Huxley (*Point Counter Point; On the Margin*); Jeffers (*Roan Stallion*); Jung (*Psychological Types*); Lardner (*Round Up; The Story of a Wonder Man; Treat 'em Rough; How to Write Short Stories*); Lawrence (*Sons and Lovers; Lady Chatterley's Lover; A Modern Lover; Mornings in Mexico; Sea and Sardinia*); Leslie (*The End of a Chapter; The Celt and the World; The Oppidan*); Lewis (*Main Street*); Lindsay (*General William Booth Enters into Heaven, and Other Poems; The Congo, and Other Poems*); A. Lowell; Mackenzie (*First Athenian Memories*); MacLeish (*The Fall of the City; Nobodaddy*); Malraux (*Man's Hope*); Masters ("Anne Rutledge"); Masefield ("Cargoes"; *Gallipoli*); Millay (*The Harp-Weaver and Other Poems*); O. Nash; G. J. Nathan (*Comedians All; Mr. George Jean Nathan Presents; The Critic and the Drama; The Theatre, the Drama, the Girls; The Intimate Notebooks*); O'Hara (*Appointment in Samarra; Butterfield 8; The Doctor's Son, and Other Stories*); O'Neill (*Strange Interlude; Anna Christie; Ah, Wilderness!; The Emperor Jones*); D. Parker (*Enough Rope; After Such Pleasures; Laments for the Living*); D. G. Phillips; Poole; Proust (*Time Regained; Within a Budding Grove; The Captive; Cities of the Plain; The Guermantes Way; The Sweet Cheat Gone*); Pound; Radiguet (*Le Bal du Comte d'Orgel*); Remarque (*All Quiet on the Western Front; Three Comrades*); Sandburg (*Abraham Lincoln*); Saroyan; Service; Sinclair (*William Fox; The Brass Check*); Stein (*Three Lives; Everybody's Autobiography; The Autobiography of Alice B. Toklas; Geography and Plays; How to Write; The Making of Americans*); Steinbeck; A. Symons; Synge (*The Playboy of the Western World; Riders to the Sea*); Tarkington (*Penrod; The Magnificent Ambersons; The Flirt*); Tate (*Mr. Pope and Other Poems*); Warren; E. Waugh (*Decline and Fall; Vile Bodies*); Wells (*God, the Invisible King*); Wescott (*The Apple of the Eye*); J. L. Weston (*From Ritual to Romance*); Wharton (*The Custom of the Country; Ethan Frome; The Age of Innocence; French Ways and Their Meaning*); Wilder (*The Cabala; The Bridge of San Luis Rey; The Angel That Troubled the Waters, and Other Plays*); W. C. Williams; E. Wilson

(*This Room and This Gin and These Sandwiches; Axel's Castle*);
Wolfe (*Look Homeward, Angel*); *The Woollcott Reader;* Yeats (*Collected Poems;* "The Lake Isle of Innisfree*").

Let me remind the reader that my investigation of Fitzgerald's reading has been based on his published canon, his notebooks, his letters, the volumes he gave to Miss Graham, the volumes he owned, and selected secondary works. Unquestionably the author read books that he did not purchase or mention; conversely, the fact that he possessed a book or referred to it is not indisputable proof he read it. I have been careful to avoid citing volumes from the two lists that have markings or signs of ownership which clearly belong to other persons (mother, wife, daughter, etc.). Let me remind the reader also that my discussion has been limited to Fitzgerald's acquaintance with literature, and even here I have been selective. He read, of course, in other fields—notably history—and in the field of literature, unlisted authors and works.

103 Kazin, pp. 201, 203.

G. Thomas Tanselle
Jackson R. Bryer

The Great Gatsby
—A Study in Literary Reputation

When the reviewer for the Boston *Transcript* commented on *The Great Gatsby* in the issue of May 23, 1925, he said that "no critic will attempt, even in the distant future, to estimate Mr. Fitzgerald's work without taking 'The Great Gatsby' into account, even though its author should create many more books." The statement is true: Fitzgerald did create many more books and we do think of *Gatsby* as Fitzgerald's central achievement. But this is not exactly what the reviewer had in mind. He was not advancing any extravagant claims for the excellence of the novel; by saying "*even* in the future," he was merely implying that *Gatsby* represents such an important development in Fitzgerald's career that it will remain historically and biographically important despite the later (and presumably greater) works that will be the full flowering of his talent. At first glance, the statement is one

Reprinted from *New Mexico Quarterly*, XXXIII (Winter 1963–64), 409-25, by permission of the authors and the publisher. © 1964 by The University of New Mexico Press.

which, read in the light of present-day opinion, may seem far-sighted and perspicacious, but which, if read in context and without the hindsight gained from years of Fitzgerald idolatry, is a typical reviewer's comment. The reviewer saw some merit in the book, to be sure, but there is no indication that his remark is anything more (or very much more) than a polite compliment, or that he had singled the book out as one which might possibly be ranked some day among the greatest works of literary art.

The fact is, of course, that it is difficult for a contemporary commentator to detect a future masterpiece—particularly when the work later comes to be thought of as a masterpiece *representative* of its times. The reviewer is likely either to dismiss the work as trivial or to say that no such people as it depicts ever existed. Fitzgerald, now regarded as the historian of the Jazz Age, was frequently criticized during his lifetime for writing about unreal characters or unbelievable situations. A book like *The Great Gatsby*, when it was praised at all, was praised for its style or its insight into American society; it was not given the kind of serious analysis it has received in the last twenty years, with emphasis on its symbolic and mythic elements. The novel may have been compared to works by Edith Wharton, Henry James, and Joseph Conrad, but it was not felt necessary to draw in Goethe, Milton, and Shakespeare, as Lionel Trilling has done. The fact that *The Great Gatsby* has been elevated to such heights serves to emphasize the mildness of the praise (and the vehemence of the criticism) with which it was received. The vicissitudes of the book's reputation form an instructive illustration of the problems involved in literary judgment. Since the book is today read in such a different way from the approach used by the contemporary reviewers (indeed in a way impossible for them), must one conclude that time is a prerequisite for the perspective needed in critical judgments? that a contemporary can never see as much in a work as a later generation can? that it is necessary to get far enough away from the period so that questions of realism in external details do not intrude?

There have been—it goes without saying—admirers of the novel from the beginning. Gertrude Stein wrote to Fitzgerald of the "genuine pleasure" the book brought her; she called it a "good book" and said he was "creating the contemporary world as much as Thackeray did his." T. S. Eliot, after referring to the novel as "charming," "overpowering," and "remarkable," declared it to be

"the first step that American fiction has taken since Henry James."
Edith Wharton wrote, "let me say at once how much I like Gatsby"; she praised the advance in Fitzgerald's technique and used
the word "masterly." And Maxwell Perkins' adjectives were "extraordinary," "magnificent," "brilliant," "unequaled"; he believed
Fitzgerald had "every kind of right to be proud of this book" full
of "such things as make a man famous" and said to him, "You
have plainly mastered the craft."

But the reviewers were not generally so enthusiastic, and several
were quite hostile. In the years following the book's publication,
there were a few critics who spoke highly of the book from time to
time, but the comments on *Gatsby* between 1925 and 1945 can
almost be counted on one's fingers, and certainly the significant
discussions require no more than the fingers of one hand. Between
1927 and the appearance of *Tender Is the Night* in 1934, there
were fewer than ten articles on Fitzgerald, and in these only three
important (though very brief) comments on *The Great Gatsby;*
between 1934 and Fitzgerald's death in 1940 there were only seven
articles, containing a few brief allusions to *Gatsby*, and one discussion in a book; in 1942 and 1943 there was one discussion each
year. In 1945, however, with the publication of essays by William
Troy and Lionel Trilling, Fitzgerald's stock was beginning to rise,
and the Fitzgerald "revival" may be said to have started. It continued at such an accelerated pace that in 1951 John Abbott Clark
wrote in the Chicago *Tribune*, "It would seem that all Fitzgerald
had broken loose." The story of the changing critical attitudes
toward *The Great Gatsby* is a study in the patterns of twentieth-
century critical fashions (since the mythic significance of the book
was discovered at the same time that the New Criticism was taking over) as well as of the (perhaps) inevitable course of events in
literary decisions. It is the success story of how "an inferior work"
with an "absurd" and "obviously unimportant" plot became a
book that "will be read as long as English literature is read anywhere."

I

When Scribner's published *The Great Gatsby* on April 10,
1925, Fitzgerald was an author with a considerable reputation,
for *This Side of Paradise* had aroused a great deal of comment five
years before and four other books had come from him since.
Gatsby, therefore, was given prominent reviews in many of the

important newspapers and journals. If it can be said in general that the most distinguished periodicals praised the book and that the attacks came from the lesser ones, it can also be said that those attacks were quite vehement and reached a large audience. For example, *Gatsby* was introduced to New Yorkers (just two days after its publication, on April 12) by the *World*, which headed its review, in large letters, "F. Scott Fitzgerald's Latest a Dud." The reviewer considered the novel "another one of the thousands of modern novels which must be approached with the point of view of the average tired person toward the movie-around-the-corner, a deadened intellect, a thankful resigning of the attention, and an aftermath of wonder that such things are produced." After discovering "no important development of . . . character" in the book, he dismissed it quickly—"with the telling of the plot 'The Great Gatsby' is, in newspaper parlance, covered."

Six days later, Ruth Hale, in the Brooklyn *Eagle*, carried the attack even farther when she wrote that she could not find "one chemical trace of magic, life, irony, romance or mysticism in all of 'The Great Gatsby' " and that Fitzgerald, whom she called "the boy,"

> is simply puttering around. It is all right as a diversion for him, probably. He does, obviously, like to use hifalutin words and hifalutiner notions to concoct these tales. There may be those who like to read him. But why he should be called an author, or why any of us should behave as if he were, has never been explained satisfactorily to me.

America went on in the same vein the next month with a very brief comment on *Gatsby* in a review of several new books: "an inferior novel, considered from any angle whatsoever . . . feeble in theme, in portraiture and even in expression." And the Springfield *Republican* (July 5, 1925) found the book "a little slack, a little soft, more than a little artificial" because "the characters . . . are blurred and incomprehensible. The 'Great Gatsby' himself . . . is unconvincing at best. Jordan . . . is the only person who stands out at all from the faintly melodramatic plot. It is a half-hearted novel that might have been composed and might better be read during a hot wave." In other words, *Gatsby* "falls into the class of negligible novels."

Other periodicals were more charitable, if rather hesitant. The *Independent* (May 2, 1925) admitted that *Gatsby* was good (better than any of Fitzgerald's earlier work except *This Side of Para-*

dise, which contained "all he knew") and that Fitzgerald was now
"over the awkward age" so that he might be able to write effectively "outside the field of sophisticated juveniles"; but his attempt at tragedy in *Gatsby* "somehow has the flavor of skimmed
milk." Similarly Walter Yust, in a review published in the New
York *Evening Post* on the same day as the *Independent's* comments, found decided weaknesses as well as strengths in the book.
Although it was a novel that "refuses to be ignored," it was at
the same time "one that reveals incredible grossness, thoughtless-
ness, polite corruption, without leaving the reader with a sense of
depression, without being insidiously provocative."

May 2 also saw the publication of another long and balanced
review, that of H. L. Mencken. He criticized the plot ("in form no
more than a glorified anecdote"):

> The story is obviously unimportant, and though, as I shall show,
> it has its place in the Fitzgerald canon, it is certainly not to be
> put on the same shelf with, say, "This Side of Paradise." What
> ails it, fundamentally, is the plain fact that it is simply a story—
> that Fitzgerald seems to be far more interested in maintaining its
> suspense than in getting under the skins of its people.

That is, except for Gatsby himself, the characters are "mere mar-
ionettes—often astonishingly lifelike, but nevertheless not quite
alive." But the book is redeemed by "the charm and beauty of the
writing," and the story, "for all its basic triviality, has a fine texture, a careful and brilliant finish. The obvious phrase is simply
not in it. . . . There is evidence in every line of hard and intelligent
effort." Fitzgerald has taken to heart the stylistic criticisms of his
earlier novels, so that now one can find pages "full of little delica-
cies, charming turns of phrase, penetrating second thoughts,"
"pages so artfully contrived that one can no more imagine improvising them than one can imagine improvising a fugue." Mencken
sees Fitzgerald the stylist challenging Fitzgerald the social historian, but he surmises that the latter is Fitzgerald's chosen role
—although Fitzgerald "does not go below the surface," he is very
accurate in his depiction of it ("The Long Island he sets before
us . . . actually exists"). When Mencken turned his attention to
Gatsby again several weeks later for his *American Mercury* column
(July 1925), he was still stressing the book's style, its "evidences
of hard, sober toil." Fitzgerald's "whole attitude," he believed,
"has changed from that of a brilliant improvisateur to that of a

painstaking and conscientious artist," and, while *Gatsby* may be "in part too well-made," it is "sound and laudable work."

At least two other reviewers were in agreement with Mencken. On April 19, Isabel Paterson had declared (in the New York *Herald Tribune*) that the novel contained "not one accidental phrase . . . nor yet one obvious or blatant line" but that Fitzgerald was not able to go beneath "the glittering surface," and that the characters "remain types." Her ambivalent conclusion was that *Gatsby* "is the first convincing testimony that Fitzgerald is . . . an artist" and at the same time that it is "a book of the season only" —but "so peculiarly of the season, that it is in its small way unique." And on May 5 the New York *Post* made the same sort of distinction between the book's style and its content: Fitzgerald demonstrates "an admirable mastery of his medium," but the "plot and its developments work out too geometrically and too perfectly for 'The Great Gatsby' to be a great novel."

When this *Post* reviewer said that Fitzgerald, with *Gatsby*, "definitely deserts his earlier fiction which brought him a lot of money and a certain kind of renown and enters into the group of American writers who are producing the best serious fiction," he was giving voice to the sort of observation that constantly reappears in these reviews—the place *Gatsby* occupies in Fitzgerald's career. Thus Llewellyn Jones, in one of the earliest reviews, believed that

> F. Scott-Fitzgerald has got his second wind, and the people who were dolefully shaking their heads over him some time ago are going to be fooled. "The Great Gatsby" is written with all the brilliancy and beauty that we associate with youth and with a sense of spiritual values that is sincere and mature. (Chicago *Evening Post*, April 17)

Similarly, the following day, Fanny Butcher commented in the Chicago *Tribune* on the implications of the new novel ("as different from the other two as experience is from innocence") for Fitzgerald's development: " 'The Great Gatsby' proves that Scott Fitzgerald is going to be a writer, and not just a man of one book. It is bizarre. It is melodramatic. It is, at moments, dime novelish. But it is, despite its faults, a book which is not negligible as any one's work, and vastly important as Scott Fitzgerald's work." Edwin Clark, in the New York *Times* the next day, felt that the novel took "a deeper look at life" than any of Fitzgerald's earlier work and showed that his sense of form "is becoming perfected." The *Literary Digest* for May found in this "graceful, finished tale" with "a kind of delicate unreality" a Fitzgerald who exhibits "a new awareness of values" and who is "no longer the impudent youngster," who is "still gay and as extravagant as ever" though "not quite as tolerant, and no longer indifferent" since he displays a new emotion, for him—pity. Carl Van Vechten, too, saw a new element in Fitzgerald in this "fine yarn, exhilaratingly spun": "a quality which has only recently made its debut in the writings of this brilliant young author, the quality vaguely referred to as mysticism" (*Nation*, May 20). The *New Yorker* (May 23) declared that the novel "has Fitzgerald's extravagance but a new maturity, as well as any amount of flash and go. . . . The young man is not petering out." And Louis Bromfield (in the August *Bookman*) believed that Fitzgerald was now "freed of the excesses of youth," since the "gaudy world" of his earlier books "has been left behind somewhere in the middle distance."

The favorable reviews not only tried to ascertain the position of *Gatsby* in Fitzgerald's career but also compared it with the work of other writers. Edwin Clark, in his *Times* review, detected a resemblance to *The Turn of the Screw*, for evil in both cases is suggested, he said, rather than made explicit. The *Bookman* (for June) compared the novel (a story of "a modern Cagliostro") with another one under review, Edith Wharton's *The Mother's Recompense*, and concluded that one "cannot deny its vitality. . . . It is Fitzgerald writing with his old gusto, with driving imagination, and with a sense of the futility of life. . . ." The *Outlook* proceeded, in July, to compare Fitzgerald's satiric catalogue of guests at Gatsby's party with Eugene Field's listing of the first families of Kentucky in his poem "The Peter-Bird" and decided (presumably on other grounds) that Fitzgerald "has serious intentions as a novelist." Early in 1926 Gilbert Seldes noted that Fitzgerald's "form is . . . derived from James through Mrs. Wharton, and there are cadences direct from the pages of Conrad"; yet Fitzgerald "has at last made his borrowings his own, and . . . they nowhere diminish the vitality of his work" (*New Criterion*, January).

This review of Seldes', with its statement that Fitzgerald "has certainly the best chance, at this moment, of becoming our finest artist in fiction," represents the opposite pole from the reaction of the *World,* which had labeled the book a "dud." Seldes' comments are a restatement of the highly favorable opinion he had expressed in the *Dial* several months earlier (August 1925), when he called *Gatsby* "one of the finest of contemporary novels." Fitzgerald, he believed, was no longer concerned only with the exterior of American life (or the "dubious tricks" of his earlier work) but has now "attacked the spirit underneath, and so has begun to report on life in its most general terms," recognizing "both his capacities and his obligations as a novelist." Conrad Aiken, reviewing the English edition in October 1926 for the *New Criterion* (where one of Seldes' reviews had appeared earlier), considered the book not "great" nor "large" nor "strikingly subtle" but nevertheless "well imagined and shaped," with a setting "admirably seized and admirably matched with the theme" and a "hard bright tone" that is "entirely original." He thought of the novel as not merely a satire, but a tragedy: Gatsby himself "comes close to being superb" as Fitzgerald reveals him to us with a "keen tenderness" that "makes his tragedy a deeply moving one."

At this pole of enthusiastic praise come also the reviews of William Rose Benét and Thomas Caldecot Chubb. Benét, in the *Saturday Review of Literature* (May 9, 1925), described *Gatsby* as "disillusioned" and "mature," with "pace" and "admirable 'control.'" Chapter Two "could not have been better written," while the catalogue of guests in Chapter Four could have been brought off by no one but Fitzgerald. Contrary to the opinions of Mencken and Isabel Paterson, Benét felt that the author has "made the real people live and breathe in all their sordidness. . . . They are memorable people of today—not types."

But it is Chubb, writing in the *Forum* (in August 1925), who probably came closer than any other reviewer to expressing the present-day attitude toward the book. Fitzgerald's "most attractive book" is "a fable in the form of a realistic novel," "at once a tragedy and an extraordinarily convincing love tale and an extravaganza. . . ." While the publishers claimed that Gatsby "would only be possible in this age and generation," Chubb felt "that he would be possible in any age and generation and impossible in all of them. . . . there is something of Jay Gatsby in every man, woman, or child that ever existed." Referring to Fitzgerald's brilliance (he "has every bit of the brilliance that we associate with hard surfaces"), Chubb asserts, "To recommend this book on the ground of technical excellence is of course superfluous. I recommend it as a study of . . . sentimentalists by one whose heart does not ever beat erratically."

The British reaction to the book in 1926 was not markedly different from the American. That is, there were those who felt, with the *Times Literary Supplement* (February 18), that it was "undoubtedly a work of art and of great promise" and those who thought the story hardly "worth the telling," an example of "[u]ndoubted talent . . . wasted on the poor material of the melodramatic corruptions of America's over-rich 'smart set' in post-war times" (*Dublin Magazine*, July-September 1926). Edward Shanks found himself on the side of the *Times*, with L. P. Hartley in the opposing camp, while the *New Statesman* (March 27) was rather noncommittal about this "satirist with a pretty thick velvet glove." Shanks, in the April *London Mercury*, said that *Gatsby* leaves "no doubt as to Mr. Fitzgerald's talents" and shows him handling "his grotesque material with an artist's discretion and . . . moderation": "Where he might well be flamboyant, he is dry; where he might be ragingly sentimental, he is full of commonsense." Hartley, on the other hand, saw in *Gatsby* only "an absurd story, whether considered as romance, melodrama, or plain record of New York high life," the work of a man whose "imagination is febrile" and whose emotion is "over-strained"; and he hoped "that Mr. Fitzgerald's heart is not in it, that it is a piece of mere naughtiness" (*Saturday Review*, February 20).

It would be a mistake to emphasize such unfavorable reviews and to say that *Gatsby* was not recognized as an excellent novel upon its appearance. The most striking characteristic of the reviews as a whole is not that they failed to praise the novel (for most of them did find something to admire in it) but that they praised it for the wrong reasons—or at least different reasons from those we now give. It was a good novel, they said, because 1) it reminded one of Conrad or James; 2) it showed an advance in Fitzgerald's artistry; 3) it had an admirable style, if not much could be said for the story; 4) it was a fine story, regardless of what one thought of the style. It was a good novel, in other words, but not extraordinary or great. Only one reviewer placed it among "the finest of contemporary novels," and only one thought of it as a "fable" and a "tragedy"; none discussed its symbolism nor its function as myth. And all their reactions perhaps serve to support Trilling's statement that "the book grows in weight of significance with the years."

II

As those years passed, *The Great Gatsby* gradually began to receive more attention, but it was not until 1945, fully twenty years after the novel's publication, that any considerable amount of serious discussion was directed toward it. In 1934 John Chamberlain was able to say (in the New York *Times* on September 20) that "many critics have been extremely discerning and loyal about 'The Great Gatsby,' " but his comment could have been based (and one must remember that the book had been out nine years) only on a handful of brief discussions (probably three) in addition to the reviews. Rebecca West, in the January 1929 *Bookman*, had called it "surely a remarkable novel" (which had "not been superseded in the common mind by better books"). Two years later Gorham Munson had remarked (October 1931 *Bookman*), almost parenthetically, "There is more art in *The Great Gatsby* than there is in the whole shelf of Mr. Dreiser's works." And Lawrence Leighton, in his 1932 *Hound and Horn* survey of the state of the American novel, had turned to *Gatsby* with "complete admiration" for Fitzgerald's "technical skill" and had found the book "worth the whole of a Dos Passos novel in its exposition of the dreariness of American life." James Gray, in two reviews of other Fitzgerald books for the St. Paul *Dispatch*, had also praised *Gatsby*—in 1926 as "a beautiful literary accomplishment" and in 1933 as "a skillful, wise and affecting book."

When Gray then wrote in 1940, "Perhaps some day it [*Gatsby*] will be rediscovered," he may have been a harbinger of what was to happen later in the decade, but he was speaking from the midst of a long period of neglect of the book—between Chamberlain's remark in 1934 and the beginning of the revival in 1945, there were no more than five or six articles that could be thought of in any way as contributing to a study of *Gatsby* (only one of them exclusively on that novel) and two or three comments in books. There had been a significant brief mention of the work in a *London Mercury* article by Harry T. Moore in March 1935, referring to *Gatsby* as "almost a great novel" and "one of the few books of the 1920's that can still stand on its feet," and Harlan Hatcher's description in the same year, in his book on modern American fiction, of the "pace and drive," "proportion and firmness of structure" of Fitzgerald's "best piece of work." James Gray had written two articles, in 1937 and 1940, the first (*Saturday Review of Literature*, June 12) pronouncing *Gatsby* Fitzgerald's "finest work" and the second (St. Paul *Dispatch*, December 24) describing it as "one of those small masterpieces which inevitably misses tremendous popular success because its implications are more subtle than the casual public cares to disentangle from a melodramatic story." There had been a few comments on *Gatsby* in the rash of articles that appeared upon Fitzgerald's death in 1940: John Dos Passos in the *New Republic* (February 17, 1941) labeling it "one of the few classic American novels," *Esquire* (for March 1941) asserting that it "will undoubtedly be read and studied a century hence," Margaret Marshall (*Nation*, February 8, 1941) believing that it "will continue to be relevant" because it "caught and crystallized the underlying 'values' of a period." And, finally, there had been Peter Quennell's study, in the *New Statesman* (February 1, 1941), of one of the book's "many virtues" ("its delineation of two rich men during the American boom"), which concluded that it is "a period piece with an unusual degree of permanent value."

As for critical books in the early forties, Oscar Cargill, in *Intellectual America* (1941), pointed out two weaknesses in what was "one of the swiftest moving of modern novels"; Alfred Kazin, in *On Native Grounds* (1942), considered *Gatsby* a "profound . . . burst of self-understanding"; and Maxwell Geismar, in *The Last of the Provincials* (1943), found it "very skillful, often superb technically, and yet curiously hollow at times." The publication of *The Last Tycoon* in 1941 even caused some critics to waver in assigning first place to *Gatsby*. Clifton Fadiman (in the *New Yorker*, November 15, 1941) called the new novel "an advance over 'The Great Gatsby' "; J. Donald Adams (New York *Times*, November 9) saw in it a "detachment" lacking in *Gatsby*, previously Fitzgerald's greatest work; and James Thurber (*New Republic*, February 9, 1942) thought that, if finished, it would rank with *Gatsby*. By 1944 (during which year virtually the only remark about *Gatsby* was J. Donald Adams'—in *The Shape of Books to Come*—that it "will be read when most of the novels of the Twenties are entirely forgotten") there was still no general agreement about Fitzgerald, even though he was beginning to be discussed in more academic journals. If Charles Weir could then view the major works (in the *Virginia Quarterly Review*) as attempts at tragedy (generally unsuccesful because Fitzgerald failed "to make the reader contemplate the problem in its larger implications"), Leo and Miriam Gurko (*College English*) could rate him "a minor writer."

All this changed abruptly, however, in 1945. In the fall of that year the publication of *The Crack-Up* was the occasion for a general reassessment, in which, even if Isidor Schneider (writing for the *New Masses*, December 4) thought *Gatsby* not fully successful, J. Donald Adams (in the September *American Mercury*) reiterated his belief that it was "one of the few American novels of the period between the wars that has some lien on posterity" and that Fitzgerald was "Hemingway's born superior." But it was in two essays by Lionel Trilling and one by William Troy that the beginnings of the revival could most clearly be seen. On August 25, Trilling reviewed *The Crack-Up* for the *Nation*, discussing Fitzgerald in relation to practically all the important writers of the past: "I am aware," he said, "that I have involved Fitzgerald with a great many great names," but he declared that the "disproportion" would not seem large to readers of "the mature work." This mature work included *Gatsby*, which New Directions reissued with an introduction by Trilling that enumerated the excellences of the book: its form, its poetic style, its grasp of "a moment of history as a great moral fact," and, above all, its hero, who "may be taken not only as an individual character but also as a symbolic or even allegorical character . . . to be thought of as standing for America itself." Troy took a similar approach in the autumn issue of *Accent*, where he termed Gatsby "one of the few truly mythological creations in our recent literature" and analyzed Fitzgerald's preoccupation with failure and his "exasperation with the multiplicity of modern human existence." Even in a brief English survey of American literature (Marcus Cunliffe's Penguin history), *Gatsby* became "a brilliant little novel . . . with a moving elegiac quality"; and for Sterling North, reviewing the *Portable Fitzgerald* in the Chicago *Sun* (October 7), the novel "dates not at all." Almost the only dissenting voice was that of Charles Poore, who judged that *Gatsby* "did not have the insight" of *This Side of Paradise* (New York *Times*, September 27).

Between 1945 and the zenith of 1951-52, commentary on the book appeared steadily, if not exactly in large quantity. In 1946 John Berryman wrote in the *Kenyon Review* that Gatsby, "a masterpiece," was "better than any other American work of fiction since *The Golden Bowl*"; James Gray, in his *On Second Thought*, referred to *Gatsby* as Fitzgerald's "best book"; and Arthur Mizener, in the *Sewanee Review*, published his first attempt at Fitzgerald biography-criticism (although, in looking at the *Portable* in the *Kenyon Review* that spring, he considered *Tender Is the Night* to be "surely Fitzgerald's most important novel"). The rest of the forties found only specialized or peripheral articles, such as Milton Hindus' discussion of anti-Semitism in Fitzgerald's portrayal of Wolfsheim (which stirred up some letters about *Gatsby* from the readers of *Commentary* in 1947), Alan Ross's analysis (in the December 1948 *Horizon*) of the relation between the man and his work (*Gatsby* being "the one novel" in which Fitzgerald "exactly and beautifully canalized the various strands of his own temperament"), Martin Kallich's 1949 study in the *University of Kansas City Review* of Fitzgerald's attitude toward wealth, D. S. Savage's general chronicle (*World Review*, August 1949) of Fitzgerald's work (in which *Gatsby* is "superlative," "a masterpiece of sympathetic understanding"), Frederick J. Hoffman's comparison (in the 1949 *English Institute Essays*) of Edith Wharton and Fitzgerald (who had "an inadequate sense of the past"), Paul L. MacKendrick's comparison of the *Satyricon* and *Gatsby* in the *Classical Journal* (both contributing to the "literature of protest"), Michael F. Moloney's critique of "half-faiths" and "social awareness" in Fitzgerald (*Catholic World*, 1950), and the January 20, 1950, *Times Literary Supplement's* survey of Fitzgerald (with *Gatsby* seen as "extraordinarily successful in blending reflection and movement").

When 1951 came, however, there was no doubt that the revival was in full swing. That year saw the production of more than thirty articles about Fitzgerald in addition to two books about him, reviews of those books, and commentary on him in still others. The most important sign of Fitzgerald's new stature was, of course, the biography by Arthur Mizener, *The Far Side of Paradise*, in which Gatsby, a "romantic," is discussed as an "embodiment of the American dream as a whole," with this dream being "the book's only positive good." Reviewers of the Mizener work also gave special mention at times to *Gatsby*. To the *TLS* (November 23, 1951), Fitzgerald "is now very generally recognized as having written in *The Great Gatsby* (1925), one of the best—if not the best—American novels of the past 50 years"; John Chamberlain in the *Freeman* (February 12) thought that *Gatsby* and *Tender Is the Night* "will be read as long as English literature is read anywhere"; and Orville Prescott in the *Times* (January 29) declared that "only a few in each generation write novels as good" as *Gatsby*, "a mature and integrated work of art." The extent of the enthusiasm is shown by the reviewer for the *Listener* (December 13): "Today, it does not seem so certain that Fitzgerald was right in thinking Hemingway the greater writer." The other book of 1951 was the collection of articles and reviews about Fitzgerald edited by Alfred Kazin, *F. Scott Fitzgerald: The Man and His Work*, which contained a number of reprinted pieces on *Gatsby* by Mencken, T. S. Eliot, and Maxwell Perkins.

Several other books that year discussed *Gatsby* as an important work of art, notably John W. Aldridge's *After the Lost Generation* (the theme of wealth), Riley Hughes in Harold C. Gardiner's *Fifty Years of the American Novel* (*Gatsby* will last because in it there is "disjunction between the author and the objects of his compassion"), Frederick J. Hoffman's *The Modern Novel in America*, and Heinrich Straumann's *American Literature in the Twentieth Century* (*Gatsby* has "an extraordinary unity of purpose in theme, plot, characterization and atmosphere"). But in general it can be said that the shorter discussions of *Gatsby* during 1951 fall into two groups: comments on *Gatsby's* relation to the man Fitzgerald, and disparaging remarks from those who disagreed with the new high valuation of Fitzgerald. Into the first category fall articles like Malcolm Cowley's "Fitzgerald: The Double Man" (*Saturday Review of Literature*, February 24), Leslie Fiedler's *New Leader* article entitled "Notes on F. Scott Fitzgerald" (which agrees that *Gatsby* is Fitzgerald's "best book"), Henry Dan Piper's analysis in Princeton's library journal of the father-image in Fitzgerald, and D. S. Savage's psychoanalytical study (in *Envoy*) of wealth and the "incest motive" in *Gatsby* and *Tender Is the Night*. The other group, the camp of the dissenters, includes Edward Dahlberg (with his caustic indictment, in the November 5 *Freeman*, of Fitzgerald's "sloven writing" and of *Gatsby*, a "novel without ideas" and an example of Fitzgerald's "peopleless realism"), Baird W. Whitlock (who wrote to the *TLS* that the "peak" of twentieth-century American literature must be "a good deal higher" than *Gatsby*), several writers of letters to the *Saturday Review of*

Literature, and Ben Ray Redman (who, in the same issue of that magazine, believed "that praise of [Fitzgerald's] work now outruns discretion").

Anyone familiar with academic criticism could predict the rest of the story. Given the facts so far—the "discovery" and elevation of a formerly underrated twentieth-century novel—the kinds of articles to follow, swept along in the giant wave of enthusiasm, conform to a pattern. There is no point in doing more than very briefly tracing this pattern since 1952. The spring of that year saw discussions of the "social thinking" in *Gatsby* (Richard Greenleaf in *Science & Society*) and of its "concern for the archetypal and essential forms of the American character and experience" (Charles Holmes in the *Pacific Spectator*); in the summer it was again studied as a "social document" (William Van O'Connor in *American Quarterly*); in the fall its symbolism and themes were treated in *College English* (by Tom Burnam); and before the end of the year its themes were scrutinized two more times, by Edwin Fussell (in *ELH*) and Henry Wechsler (in the Washington and Jefferson *Wall*). Through 1953, 1954, and 1955 many important critics turned their attention to the book, discussing it in terms of its commentary on money (Malcolm Cowley in the *Western Review*, 1953), its mythology (Douglas Taylor in the *University of Kansas City Review*, 1953), its criticism of America (Marius Bewley in the *Sewanee Review*, 1954), its theme of "time confused and disordered" (Robert Wooster Stallman in *Modern Fiction Studies*, 1955), even its telephone symbolism (B. B. Cohen in the Indiana *Folio*, 1954), bringing in comparisons with Benjamin Franklin (Floyd Watkins in the *New England Quarterly* and Hugh Maclean in *College English*, 1954), Dickens (Norman Friedman in *Accent*, 1954), T. S. Eliot (John Bicknell in the *Virginia Quarterly Review*, 1954), Conrad (Robert Stallman in *Twentieth Century Literature*, 1955), and Sophocles' Oedipus (Hans Meyerhoff's *Time in Literature*). Frederick J. Hoffman, who felt *Gatsby* was "a sentimental novel," also believed that its "details are presented with brilliantly accurate insight, greater than any other found in modern American literature" (*The Twenties*, 1955); R. F. Richards, in a 1955 "dictionary" of American literature, discerned in it "one of the most perfect structures in literature"; Robert Spiller, in his *Cycle of American Literature* (1955), thought it Fitzgerald's "most finished novel"; and Louis Untermeyer (in his Fitzgerald

chapter of *Makers of the Modern World*) talked of its "unforgettable" scenes and "universal" implications.
In the late fifties there was no slackening of the pace. The comparisons continued—with Hemingway (Arthur Mizener in the fifteenth *Perspectives U.S.A.*), Conrad again (Jerome Thale in *Twentieth Century Literature*, 1957), and Dreiser (Eric Solomon in *Modern Language Notes*, 1958)—and there were studies focused on the narrator, Nick Carraway (Thomas Hanzo in *Modern Fiction Studies*, 1957), the theme of the "unending quest of the romantic dream" (Robert Ornstein in *College English*, 1956), and of reality versus imagination (Don Wahlquist in *Inland*, 1957), the language of the book (W. J. Harvey in *English Studies*, 1957), its use of legends and myth (John Henry Raleigh in the *University of Kansas City Review*, June and October 1957, and Richard Chase in his *American Novel and Its Tradition*), its blending of "the abstract, the ideal, and the mythical" with a "realistic treatment of our culture" (J. R. Kuehl in *Texas Studies*, 1959), its pattern and structure (John W. Aldridge in Charles Shapiro's collection of *Twelve Original Essays on Great American Novels*), and the symbolism of Dr. Eckleberg's eyes (Milton Hindus in *Boston University Studies in English*, 1957) and of noses (John C. Weston in *Fitzgerald Newsletter*, 1959). By 1958 Matthew J. Bruccoli was able to say (in the *Newsletter*) that Fitzgerald "is still the most consistently underrated American writer," even though, the year before, James E. Miller had published a full-length monograph on Fitzgerald's technique (including a detailed discussion of *Gatsby*) and that year the Bodley Head in London began reprinting Fitzgerald's work (with an introduction by J. B. Priestley). Also in 1958 some uncollected material was gathered together as *Afternoon of an Author*, which provoked from the London *Times* (on October 9) the obiter dictum that *Gatsby* "has a significance that can be accorded to few American books written between the wars." In 1959 Peter Munro Jack gave *Gatsby* a place in the "James Branch Cabell period" (in Malcolm Cowley's collection, *After the Genteel Tradition*); Frederick E. Faverty (in *Your Literary Heritage*) praised the book's realism, its technique, and its "arresting" symbolism; and Mizener, in a new paperback edition of his biography, compared *Gatsby* to Stendhal's *Le Rouge et le Noir*.
By 1960 *Gatsby* was without doubt thought of as a classic, so that no one was surprised to find it discussed in works with such

broad titles as J. B. Priestley's *Literature and Western Man* or
Leon Howard's *Literature and the American Tradition*, and Arthur
Mizener found it in order to survey in the New York *Times*
(April 24) some of the earlier criticism (concluding that only re-
cently had "the obvious values" of the novel "been reasonably
established"). From J. S. Westbrook's explication of the novel in
American Literature in 1960, through Richard C. Carpenter's in
the *Explicator* in 1961, Charles E. Shain's 1961 pamphlet in the
Minnesota series, and the entire issue of *Modern Fiction Studies*
(Spring 1961) devoted to Fitzgerald (with two articles on *Gatsby*), down to Andrew Turnbull's biography and the whole volume
of material about *Gatsby* edited by Frederick J. Hoffman in 1962
(including Henry Dan Piper's discussion of the religious background of the novel), academic criticism has shown no sign of
declining. Within the last year alone there have been detailed
treatments of the novel in books about Fitzgerald (Kenneth Eble
takes up its structure and "romantic vision," William Goldhurst
its relation to the work of Mencken, Hemingway, Lardner, and
Edmund Wilson) and articles on its "statement and technique"
(Michael Millgate in *Modern Language Review*), its "imagery and
meaning" (Guy Owen in *Stetson Studies*), its use of the grotesque
(Howard Babb in *Criticism*), of "the artifact in imagery" (M.
Bettina in *Twentieth Century Literature*), and of Platonic thought
(Paul Lauter in *Modern Fiction Studies*). When one looks back
over the seventy-five or more articles and chapters that have, since
1950, been wholly or partially devoted to *Gatsby*, one has no difficulty in agreeing with Charles Shain's statement that *Gatsby* "has
been discussed and admired as much as any twentieth-century
American novel." And when, on top of that, one looks at the dozen
or so doctoral dissertations that discuss the book and the articles
and books in French, Italian, German, Dutch, and Swedish, one is
likely—if not totally overwhelmed—to have some disquieting
thoughts.

Of course, doubts about the "revival" did go along with the
enthusiasm—there is always the minority report. If Martin Schock-
ley's decision in his 1954 *Arizona Quarterly* article that it was
time to "place upon Fitzgerald's brow the small and wilted laurel
that is his" seems too harsh, Albert J. Lubell made the same point
more temperately the next year in the *South Atlantic Quarterly*
when he asserted that the "recent criticism of [Fitzgerald], attempting to correct the wrong of his undue neglect, itself needs a

corrective." And P. K. Elkin, in the *Australian Quarterly* of June 1957, praised *Gatsby* very highly, but not until he had pointed out how a great deal of the revival had "obscured" Fitzgerald's "more substantial attributes." But the dissenters are a part of the general enthusiasm, and it goes without saying that any such revival of interest in a work of literature is not based entirely on cool and balanced judgment. In 1961 (for a summer reading issue of the New York *Herald Tribune's* book review) Jerome Weidman listed *Gatsby* as one of his seven favorite books because "it catches, better than anything I have ever read, heard, or can remember, the extraordinary time during which I grew up and, to return to its meticulously written pages strewn with incandescent images that grow brighter with the years, is to be again a part of that time." His statement perhaps explains the revival as well as anything does.

More is involved here than the question of whether contemporaries can accurately judge a work of art—or, indeed, whether we are still (only two generations after *Gatsby* appeared) too close to have perspective. There is more involved than the question of how accurate *Gatsby* is in portraying a particular period. It is rather a matter of the way we look back at that period and of the values we place on certain kinds of criticism. How often do our sentimental and nostalgic feelings determine our critical reactions? How often is a literary judgment self-perpetuating? An examination of the reputation of *The Great Gatsby* may serve as an index to the critical taste of the last forty years; but, beyond that, it is a case study in the workings of literary evaluation—of the critical snowballing process by which a work becomes established as a classic. Such an inquiry is disturbing, not in the sense that every subjective value judgment leaves room for doubts, but because one begins to feel that this process follows a pattern, that it has become mechanical, that a great deal of energy may have been misdirected. This is not to say that *Gatsby* does not deserve the attention it has received. It is merely a way of saying that *Gatsby* has provided us with more than one fable—that the story of its reception is itself a parable showing up what is best and what is worst in recent criticism.

Matthew J. Bruccoli

Tender is the Night
—Reception and Reputation

Reception

It dealt with fashionable life in the 1920s at a time when most
readers wanted to forget that they had ever been concerned with
frivolities; the new fashion was for novels about destitution and
revolt. . . . most reviewers implied that it belonged to the bad old
days before the crash. . . . [Malcolm Cowley][1]

Tender is the Night was published on April 12, 1934.[2] Considering the expectation that had been aroused by F. Scott Fitzgerald's
nine-year pause after *The Great Gatsby*, the reviews of the new
novel were unemotional. In the June number of the *North American Review*, Herschel Brickell mentioned "the kind of violent argument that has been going on about it"; since there was no real
controversy in print—only disagreement—this argument must
have raged among readers. It has continued, and the publication
in 1951 of Malcolm Cowley's edition of the "author's final version"

Reprinted and revised from Matthew J. Bruccoli, *The Composition of
Tender is the Night* (Pittsburgh: University of Pittsburgh Press, 1963),
pp. 1-16, by permission of the author and the publisher.

stimulated the debate. Inevitably, the discussions of *Tender is the Night* return to the critical reception of the novel, a subject which includes some folklore.

One of the commonplaces of Fitzgerald criticism is that *Tender is the Night* failed in 1934 because the reviewers ganged up on it and ridiculed the book as an anachronistic hang-over from the twenties. These reviewers, so the story goes, compounded their socio-political prejudice with obtuseness by pretending to find extraordinary difficulty in the elementary flashback structure. The reviewers were allegedly abetted by the reading public, which rejected Fitzgerald and turned its attention to escapism or social tracts. Depending upon whether one is listening to an anti-revisionist or a revisionist, this conspiracy between the critics and the public is supposed to have either so befuddled Fitzgerald's critical abilities that he desperately reorganized the novel in straight chronological order—or to have revealed to him what was wrong with *Tender is the Night* so that he could correct its structural flaws. The winds of favor are blowing in the direction of the original version.

Like most of the biographical-critical stories about Fitzgerald, the *Tender* story is an intriguing pattern of fact and lugubrious balderdash. It is true that Fitzgerald's most ambitious novel was a failure in its own time; and it is true that its reception hurt Fitzgerald, and doubtlessly contributed to his crack-up. But it is not demonstrable that Fitzgerald was the victim of a hostile, New-Deal oriented press. In all fairness, the assassination of *Tender is the Night* cannot be added to the catalogue of the Democrats' iniquities. The majority of the notices were favorable, and there was little outcry against the jazz-age material and the flashback. That some of the favorable reviews tended to patronize Fitzgerald is certainly true, but critics had patronized him when stocks were high.

A glance at the ten best-selling novels of 1934 provides nothing to suggest that the readers of the Depression rejected Fitzgerald because they preferred socially significant novels about slums: *Anthony Adverse; Lamb in his Bosom; So Red the Rose; Good-Bye, Mr. Chips; Within This Present; Work of Art; Private Worlds; Mary Peters; Oil for the Lamps of China;* and *Seven Gothic Tales.* This is a typical mixture, and there is not one proletarian novel in the lot. Indeed, *Within This Present* is a nostalgic look back at the twenties. That the three top sellers of the year were historical novels, and that the number four book was *Good-Bye, Mr. Chips* may indicate a streak of escapism in the reading public; but historical novels and sentimental books about school-masters sell well, boom or bust.

People who lament the failure of *Tender is the Night* generally ignore the fact that Fitzgerald had not had a best seller since *This Side of Paradise*, and even it was not one of the top ten in 1920. Fitzgerald was a popular figure, but he was never really a popular novelist in his lifetime. *The Great Gatsby*, one of the great novels written in this country, was a comparative flop in 1925, selling only about 25,000 copies. Yet we infrequently hear laments about the popular failure of that novel. Between the serialization in *Scribner's Magazine* and the 13,000 copies of *Tender is the Night* sold in 1934-35, it probably reached as many readers as did *The Great Gatsby*.

Sixty-four reviews of *Tender* have been located.[3] Ten prominent reviewers reacted favorably—including John Chamberlain, C. Hartley Grattan, and Herschel Brickell. Six were more favorable than not—including Horace Gregory, Clifton Fadiman, and the *Times Literary Supplement*. Eight were clearly unfavorable—including William Troy, Lewis Gannett, and Peter Quennell. Only six specifically discuss the flashback, and those split evenly on it. Four reviews take exception to the expatriate material from the twenties. The most interesting fact is that eight reviews criticize the credibility of Dick Diver or the convincingness of his crack-up. In the week following publication of *Tender is the Night*, John Chamberlain commented in the *New York Times* on the mixed reactions of his colleagues: "The critical reception of F. Scott Fitzgerald's *Tender is the Night* might serve as the basis for one of those cartoons on 'Why Men Go Mad.' No two reviews were alike; no two had the same tone. Some seemed to think that Mr. Fitzgerald was writing about his usual jazz age boys and girls; others that he had a 'timeless' problem on his hands. And some seemed to think that Doctor Diver's collapse was insufficiently documented."

The jazz-age material was attacked by *News-Week*, which headlined its review with "A Sinful, Ginful Tale" and noted that "It is a long time since the decay of American expatriates on the Riviera was hot news." But the socially conscious *New Republic* did not harass Fitzgerald about his choice of material. Reviewer Malcolm Cowley developed a sober analysis of Fitzgerald's apparent indecision between writing a psychological or a social novel

—Fitzgerald thought of it as a dramatic novel—and then Cowley proposed a theory that has since gained favor, the theory that as the novel developed through several versions, the early sections crystallized so that the author was not able to make them harmonize with the later sections. Bluntly stated, this is the view that the novel was rewritten to death.

The *New York Times* reviewed *Tender is the Night* three times. First, Chamberlain covered it in his daily book column on April 13, in an extremely favorable notice which makes only the criticism that the reader is puzzled by the abrupt dismissal of Rosemary at the end of Book I. This criticism is immediately qualified by the statement, "At this point one could almost guarantee that *Tender is the Night* is going to be a failure. But, as a matter of fact, the novel does not really begin until Rosemary is more or less out of the way." This review was followed by a lukewarm one in the Sunday *New York Times Book Review* by J. Donald Adams, who felt that Nicole and Rosemary were unconvincing characters and that Dick's crack-up was contrived. On the following day Chamberlain interrupted a review of Faulkner's *Doctor Martino* to defend the integrity of Dick's characterization. It is impossible to avoid the conclusion that this comment was a rejoinder to Adams. After explaining how Fitzgerald had carefully documented Dick's collapse, Chamberlain concluded with a wry observation: "This seems to us to be a sufficient exercise in cause-and-effect. Compared to the motivation in Faulkner, it is logic personified." However, a third of the reviews I have checked echo Adams' opinion; Henry Seidel Canby, Clifton Fadiman, and William Troy, among others, concurred.

D. W. Harding went even further and asserted that Fitzgerald had not supplied any cause for Dick's crack-up. His review is puzzling, for he protests that he had been moved against his will by Dick's decline, and concludes by unconsciously echoing Fitzgerald's style: ". . . I am prepared to be told that this attempt at analysis is itself childish—an attempt to assure myself that the magician didn't really cut the lady's head off, did he? I still believe there was a trick in it." The most comprehensive defense of Dick's decline and of the novel's structure was made by C. Hartley Grattan in the *Modern Monthly*. That Grattan was defending Fitzgerald against other critics is clear from a comment on Dick's final pilgrimage into obscurity: "This fate is so close to that of unstable personalities in any place and time that it has been perversely misread by those critics anxious to avoid the implications of the whole book." The attacks on the verisimilitude of Dick's decline appear to have troubled Fitzgerald more than anything else the critics wrote. He resented the implication that he had been clumsy and that he had lost control of his material. On April 23, eleven days after date of publication, Fitzgerald wrote to H. L. Mencken to break an engagement and then added an emotional defense of Book III of *Tender is the Night*:

> Without wanting to add to your mass of accumulated correspondence just as you've cleared it away, I would like to say in regard to my book that there was a deliberate intention in every part of it except the first. The first part, the romantic introduction, was too long and too elaborated, largely because of the fact that it had been written over a series of years with varying plans, but everything else in the book conformed to a *definite intention* and if I had to start to write it again tomorrow I would adopt the same plan, irrespective of the fact of whether I had, in this case, brought it off or not brought it off. That is what most of the critics fail to understand (outside of the fact that they fail to recognize and identify anything in the book) that the motif of the "dying fall" was absolutely deliberate and did not come from any diminution of vitality, but from a definite plan.
>
> That particular trick is one that Ernest Hemingway and I worked out—probably from Conrad's preface to "The Nigger"—and it has been the greatest "credo" in my life, ever since I decided that I would rather be an artist than a careerist. I would rather impress my image (even though an image the size of a nickel) upon the soul of a people than be known, except in so far as I have my natural obligation to my family—to provide for them. I would as soon be as anonymous as Rimbaud, if I could feel that I had accomplished that purpose—and that is no sentimental yapping about being disinterested. It is simply that having once found the intensity of art, nothing else that can happen in life can ever again seem as important as the creative process.[4]

The letter suggests that Fitzgerald's later decision to revise the structure of the novel was not prompted by the desire to circumvent the possible confusion caused by the flashback. The removal of the flashback was the result of Fitzgerald's desire to emphasize the documentation of Dick's decline by putting together all the information about him. Fitzgerald hoped thereby to make it more apparent that Dick's decline was the result of certain long-standing tensions in his personality. The new structure would also make Dick's final collapse seem less abrupt. The problem was on Fitzgerald's mind in 1938 when he was trying to persuade Maxwell Perkins to bring out an omnibus volume of his novels. Fitzgerald was particularly anxious to give *Tender is the Night* another chance, and remarked that: "Its great fault is that the *true* beginning—the young psychiatrist in Switzerland—is tucked away in the middle of the book."[5] This view of the novel seems to have resulted from a straw vote Fitzgerald took. An inscribed copy he gave to Joseph Hergesheimer reveals Fitzgerald's particular concern about the reactions of fellow writers.[6]

Dear Joe:
   You talked to someone who didn't like this book—I don't know who, or why they didn't. But I could tell in the Stafford Bar that afternoon when you said it was "almost impossible to write a book about an actress" that you hadn't read it thru because the actress fades out of it in the first third + is only a catalytic agent.
   Sometime will you open it at the middle, perhaps at page 155 + read on for five or ten minutes—? If it were not for my sincere admiration for your judgement I would forgo this plea. You were not the only one repelled by the apparent triviality of the opening—I would like this favorite among my books to have another chance in the chrystal light of your taste
                                               Ever yrs
                                         F Scott Fitzgerald
   Page 155—*et sq.*

Publicly, at least, Fitzgerald tried to show that he was not greatly disturbed by the reviews. When later in the year he was asked to prepare an introduction to the Modern Library edition of *The Great Gatsby*, he used it as an opportunity to discuss his critics. Though the essay ostensibly deals with *The Great Gatsby*, it is immediately clear that Fitzgerald is referring obliquely to the reception of *Tender is the Night*. Pretending to be indifferent to critical onslaughts, Fitzgerald at first adopts a tough tone: "Your pride is all you have, and if you let it be tampered with by a man who has a dozen prides to tamper with before lunch, you are promising yourself a lot of disappointments that a hard-boiled professional has learned to spare himself." But this shifts to bitter indignation in which Fitzgerald makes a profound comment on his career. "But, my God! it was my material, and it was all I had to deal with."[7]

Reputation

Although next to nothing was written about *Tender is the Night* during the thirties, the book was not wholly forgotten. There was a feeling of uneasiness about it, a suspicion that perhaps it had not been fairly treated. "A strange thing is that in retrospect his *Tender is the Night* gets better and better," Ernest Hemingway commented to Maxwell Perkins.[8] This feeling was shared by Peter Monro Jack, who wrote in 1937, "*Tender is the Night* is a ghost wandering by its former triumphs. But instead of crying Revenge! it is still wondering why it was so foully murdered. . . . As one reads *Tender is the Night*, with its charming and evocative writing, one feels how badly Fitzgerald was served by his contemporaries."[9] The friendly articles occasioned by Fitzgerald's death in 1940 concentrated on *The Great Gatsby*, but the publication of *The Crack-Up* in 1945 resulted in a number of reassessments of Fitzgerald's career. In these articles *Tender is the Night* was generally treated with uneasy respect: it was recognized as having brilliance, though these critics followed the lead of the 1934 reviews in citing the novel's structural difficulties or the lack of verisimilitude in the characterization of Dick Diver. In general, the 1945 estimates of *Tender is the Night* indicate that a re-evaluation of the novel was developing; there is a hesitancy to be detected in some of these articles, which indicates that the writers are unwilling to commit themselves just yet. An example is this remark by Alfred Kazin: "But Fitzgerald is one of those novelists whom it is easier to appreciate than to explain, and whom it is possible, even fascinating to read over and over—it has often been remarked that *Tender is the Night* grows better on each re-reading —without always being able to account for the sources of your pleasure."[10]

The publication in 1951 of Cowley's edition of "the author's final version" naturally focused attention on the structural problem. Cowley argued that "the author's final version" is a decided improvement over the 1934 version because the novel now concentrates the reader's attention on Dick Diver and his tragedy:

One fault of the earlier version was its uncertainty of focus. We weren't quite sure in reading it whether the author had intended to write about a whole group of Americans on the Riviera—that is, to make the book a social study with a collective hero—or whether he had intended to write a psychological novel about the glory and decline of Richard Diver as a person.[11]

This comment is not a rationalization that Cowley invented in 1951 to defend his edition, for it echoes his 1934 review of *Tender is the Night*. Nonetheless, Cowley's feeling that the novel wants focus is puzzling because the 1934 version is clearly Dick's book. His friends are important only as reflector characters. The revisionist and anti-revisionist receptions of Cowley's version were about equally strong. But rather than maintaining interest in the structural problem, this edition seems to have ultimately killed interest in the problem. The explanation for this reaction would seem to be that readers recognized that the revised structure did not really have a significant effect on the essential qualities of *Tender is the Night*.

Interest in the revisions gradually diminished until in 1960 Scribners selected the original version for its paperback textbook series. The diminution of interest in the structural problems of *Tender is the Night* has caused interest to shift to other aspects of the novel—mainly in the areas of psychology and sociology. More and more attention has been given to the novel's arraignment of American civilization, and these comments have been predominantly laudatory. In a thoughtful article on Fitzgerald's insights into American life, Edwin S. Fussell states: "The social structure of *Tender is the Night* is epic in scope and intention, though it has the grace and concentration of lyric. . . ." He goes on to explain that Fitzgerald's analysis of society operates on four levels in *Tender is the Night*.[12]

Another critic who sees *Tender is the Night* as a continuation of *The Great Gatsby's* arraignment of the American success ethos is Otto Friedrich, who comments, "Yet in spite of its faults, *Tender is the Night* is unquestionably a great novel. While *The Great Gatsby* represents Fitzgerald's most perfectly expressed insight into the fraud of his own dream of success, *Tender is the Night* combines that new insight with a new understanding of how and why the dream disintegrates."[13]

Less happy are the studies inspired by the psychological aspects of *Tender is the Night*. Although it is not specifically a novel about a psychologist or even a psychological novel, this subject matter has inevitably generated considerable interest. Comments range from Robert Stanton's comparatively conservative attempt to demonstrate that *Tender is the Night* is unified by "incest-motifs" (the term is used loosely enough to cover love between a mature man and a younger woman) which symbolize both "Dick's loss of allegiance to the moral code of his father" and "a social situation existing throughout Europe and America during the Twenties"—to D. S. Savage's statement that "The incest motive is in fact central to all of Fitzgerald's novels" and Maxwell Geismar's view that "Fitzgerald's work, like Poe's, is colored by the imagery of incest."[14] Leslie Fiedler views the novel as presenting sexual ambiguities in which the male and female characters exchange roles.[15]

Interesting as the comments on the social and incestuous aspects of *Tender is the Night* are—and the former is indubitably a valid approach to the novel—the book is principally concerned with Dick Diver's tragedy; and there continues to be a strong body of opinion that he is not a credible figure and that his collapse seems unconvincing or insufficiently documented. This criticism almost always argues that Fitzgerald confused his own tragedy with Dick's and consequently, in Friedrich's words, "fell into the old trap of ascribing his own experiences to largely unrelated causes that he provided for the sake of plot." A representative attack on the characterization of Dick was included in Albert Lubell's 1955 protest against the Fitzgerald revival:

> Not that a novelist can spell out the causes of a character's disintegration in the clinical manner of a psychiatrist. But he can, and should, provide us with a key to the understanding of a character, which should show us why the character did what he did or suffered what he suffered. This key to the understanding of Dick Diver, Fitzgerald in the end has failed to give. Thus Fitzgerald's failure in *Tender is the Night* is fundamentally a failure to objectify his material and to fuse its "layers of experience" into an artistically unified whole.[16]

Obviously, any critic's reaction to the depiction of Dick Diver must be fundamentally personal. The critic who finds Dick Diver an unconvincing or confusing character will not be persuaded otherwise by any amount of argument—or by a detailed reconstruction of the composition of *Tender is the Night.* For the record, this reader believes that Dick Diver is a satisfying character, that the causes of his deterioration are sufficiently probed, that his fall is moving, and that the novel is unified by Fitzgerald's view of his hero. A study of the manuscripts supports some of these beliefs. Although Fitzgerald did not write long, detailed analyses of his work, the preliminary sketch of Dick Diver prepared in 1932 indicates that he knew the causes of Dick's decline. The first holograph draft for the published version of *Tender is the Night* reveals that Fitzgerald felt he thoroughly understood his hero. There are no discarded sections which show contradictory views of Dick Diver. This evidence, admittedly negative, is supplemented by the revisions of the typed drafts in which Fitzgerald points up his interpretation of his protagonist.

The alleged confusion in Fitzgerald's treatment of Dick Diver is frequently connected with the alleged confusion in the structure of *Tender is the Night.* Again the evidence is mainly negative: there is no other discarded structure, and there is no indication that Fitzgerald had any doubts about his narrative plan while he was writing the novel. But there is also the author's summary of Book III in which he flatly states that the withdrawal of Dick Diver from the center of the narrative, which has puzzled some critics, was the intended effect: "All Dick's stories such as are *absolutely necessary* . . . must be told without putting in his reactions or feelings. From now on he is mystery man, at least to Nicole with her guessing at the mystery."[17]

It is not easy to comprehend the basis of the complaints about the narrative difficulty of *Tender is the Night,* which involves one flashback sequence and three obvious shifts in point of view. Its plotting is less elaborate than that of *The Great Gatsby* and is far less complex than the novels of James and Conrad. Indeed, Fitzgerald esteemed Conrad as the greatest literary artist of the time and carefully studied him. Fitzgerald informed Mencken that the "dying fall" technique in *Tender is the Night* was taken from Conrad. It is likely that the theory behind the narrative plan of *Tender is the Night* was also learned from Conrad. Although Fitzgerald probably learned his lessons studying Conrad's novels, he may have read Ford Madox Ford's formulation of the theory in *Joseph Conrad: A Personal Remembrance* (1924):

> For it became very early evident to us that what was the matter with the Novel and the British novel in particular, was that it

went straight forward, whereas in your gradual making acquaint-
anceship with your fellows you never do go straight forward. You
meet an English gentleman at your golf club. He is beefy, full of
health, the moral of the boy from an English Public School of the
finest type. You discover, gradually, that he is hopelessly neuras-
thenic, dishonest in matters of small change, but unexpectedly
self-sacrificing. . . . To get such a man in fiction you could not
begin at his beginning and work his life chronologically to the
end. You must first get him in with a strong impression, and then
work backwards and forwards over his past.[18]

This is the method Fitzgerald selected for Dick Diver—and for
the same reasons given by Ford. It is not new or esoteric, and it
certainly did not originate with Conrad. Fitzgerald's complication
of presenting his opening sequence through the starry eyes of
Rosemary Hoyt also has solid precedents. Again, it is not a particularly difficult device. If it fails in *Tender is the Night*, it does so
not because the device itself is confusing, but because Fitzgerald's
use of it is maladroit. Perhaps the criticism that the reader is
puzzled at the end of Book I when he discovers that the novel is
not about Rosemary can be taken as an indication of the skill with
which Fitzgerald has developed her point of view.

NOTES

1. *Tender is the Night*, "The Author's Final Version," ed. Malcolm
Cowley (New York, 1951), p. x.
2. It had been serialized in four installments of *Scribner's Magazine*
(January-April, 1934). Popular and critical reactions to the serial
seem to have been tepid. The mood and structure of the novel were
not suited to month-long interruptions, and serialization hurt the sale
and reception of the book. Fitzgerald was concerned about the effect
of serialization; he wrote in the copy of *Tender* he gave to Dorothy
Parker: "Dear Dotty This is better than the magazine" (Collection of
Matthew J. Bruccoli).
3. Anonymous. "Decadence: Fitzgerald Again Tells a Sinful, Ginful
Tale," *News-Week*, III (April 14, 1934), 39-40.
_____. "A New Fitzgerald," *Princeton Alumni Weekly*, XXXIV
(May 4, 1934), 665.
_____. Review of *Tender Is the Night*, *Journal of Nervous and
Mental Disease*, LXXXII (July 1935), 115-17.
_____. "Scott Fitzgerald Essays Return to Novel Writing," *Mil-
waukee Journal*, April 22, 1934, Sec. V., p. 3.
_____. "Sophisticates Abroad," *Time*, XXIII (April 16, 1934), 77.

_____. " 'Tender Is the Night,' " *Springfield* (Mass.) *Sunday Union and Republican,* April 29, 1934, p. 7E.

A[dams], J. D[onald]. "Scott Fitzgerald's Return to the Novel," *New York Times Book Review,* April 15, 1934, p. 7.

Anderson, Katherine McClure. "Today's Book," *Macon Telegraph,* April 11, 1934, p. 4.

Beck, Clyde. "The Doctor and the Movie Star," *Detroit News,* April 14, 1934, p. 20.

Borland, Hal. " 'Of Making Many Books—,' " *Philadelphia Public Ledger,* April 13, 1934, p. 9.

Brickell, Herschel. "Americans Abroad," *North American Review,* CCXXXVII (June 1934), 569-70.

_____. "Books on our Table," *New York Post,* April 14, 1934, p. 13.

Butcher, Fanny. "New Fitzgerald Book Brilliant; Fails as Novel," *Chicago Tribune,* April 14, 1934, p. 10.

Canby, Henry Seidel. "In the Second Era of Demoralization," *Saturday Review of Literature,* X (April 14, 1934), 630-31.

Chamberlain, John. "Books of The Times," *New York Times,* April 13, 1934, p. 17.

_____. "Books of The Times," *New York Times,* April 16, 1934, p. 15.

Clarage, Eleanor. Review of *Tender Is the Night, Cleveland Plain Dealer,* April 13, 1934, p. 7.

Coleman, Arthur. "Fitzgerald's Stature Is Increased by His Novel About Americans in France," *Dallas Morning News,* April 15, 1934, Sec. III, p. 10.

Colum, Mary M. "The Psychopathic Novel," *Forum and Century,* XCI (April 1934), 219-23.

Cowley, Malcolm. "Breakdown," *New Republic,* LXXIX (June 6, 1934), 105-6.

Daniel, Frank. " 'Tender Is the Night,' " *Atlanta Journal,* May 20, 1934, Magazine Section, p. 14.

Diamant, Gertrude. "Child Prodigy," *American Mercury,* XXXIII (October 1934), 249-51.

Fadiman, Clifton. "F. Scott Fitzgerald," *New Yorker,* X (April 14, 1934), 112-15.

G., C.M. "F. Scott Fitzgerald: Fitzgerald Follows the Times in Complicated Tale," *Albany Knickerbocker Press,* May 13, 1934, Sec. 4, p. 7.

Gannett, Lewis. "Books and Things," *New York Herald Tribune,* April 13, 1934, p. 15.

Grattan, C. Hartley. Review of *Tender Is the Night, Modern Monthly,* VIII (July 1934), 375-77.

Gray, James. "Fitzgerald Re-Enters, Leading Bewildered Giant," *St. Paul Dispatch,* April 12, 1934, Sec. I, p. 8.

Gray, James. "Fitzgerald Serial Improves Greatly As Story Advances," *St. Paul Dispatch,* January 18, 1934, p. 6.

Gregory, Horace. "A Generation Riding To Romantic Death," *New York Herald Tribune Book Review,* April 15, 1934, p. 5.

Hansen, Harry. "The First Reader," *New York World-Telegram,* April 12, 1934, p. 25.

Hart, Philomena. "Among the Lost People of Three Notable Volumes," *Providence Sunday Journal,* April 22, 1934, Sec. E, p. 4.

Lewis, Gordon. "Scott Fitzgerald Is Author of New Novel," *Charlotte News,* May 6, 1934, Sec. II, p. 9.

Loveman, Amy. Review of *Tender Is the Night, Saturday Review of Literature,* X (April 7, 1934), 610.

M., M. "Moved by Futility," *Los Angeles Times,* May 6, 1934, Part II, p. 7.

MacMillan, H. A. "Mr. Fitzgerald Displays His Little White Mice," *St. Paul Daily News,* April 22, 1934, Magazine Section, p. 4.

March, D'Arcy. "Ebb Tide," *Canadian Forum,* XIV (July 1934), 404.

March, Michael. "Page After Page," *Brooklyn Citizen,* April 11, 1934, p. 11.

Murphy, Spencer. "Scott Fitzgerald Develops Novel Idea In His Latest Book," *Charlotte Observer,* May 20, 1934, Section Three, p. 8.

O., H. "Psychiatrist and Patient," *Baltimore Evening Sun,* April 21, 1934, p. 6.

P., S. "Psychiatrist," *Cincinnati Enquirer,* April 28, 1934, p. 7.

Patterson, Curtis. "Pathology Rears Its Ugly Head," *Town & Country,* LXXXIX (April 15, 1934), 42, 70.

Peterson, G. L. "The Booking Office," *Minneapolis Tribune,* May 6, 1934, Sec. (3), p. 11.

Potter, Merle. "Americans In Other Lands," *Minneapolis Journal,* April 15, 1934, Editorial Section, p. 7.

Quennell, Peter. Review of *Tender Is the Night, New Statesman and Nation,* n.s. VII (April 28, 1934), 642.

Rahv, Philip. "You Can't Duck Hurricane Under a Beach Umbrella," *Daily Worker* (New York), May 5, 1934, p. 7.

Rascoe, Burton. "Esquire's Five-Minute Shelf," *Esquire,* I (April 1934), 133, 159, 161, 162-63.

Riley, Edith Carl. *"Tender Is the Night,"* *Houston Post,* April 15, 1934, Sec. 2, p. 9.

Rogers, Cameron. "Fitzgerald's Novel a Masterpiece," *San Francisco Chronicle,* April 15, 1934, p. 4D.

Seldes, Gilbert. "True to Type—Scott Fitzgerald Writes Superb Tragic Novel," *New York Evening Journal,* April 12, 1934, p. 23.

Troy, William. "The Worm i' the Bud," *The Nation*, CXXXVIII (May 9, 1934), 539-40.

Wagner, Charles A. "Books," *New York Sunday Mirror*, April 15, 1934, p. 24.

Walley, Harold R. "The Book Worm's Turn," *Ohio State Journal* (Columbus), June 6, 1934, p. 5.

Walton, Edith H. Review of *Tender Is the Night, Forum and Century*, XCI (June 1934), iv.

_____. "Stale; Unprofitable," *New York Sun*, April 14, 1934, p. 30.

Weeks, Edward. Review of *Tender Is the Night, Atlantic Monthly*, CLIII (April 1934), 17.

Wilson, Rowena. "Scott Fitzgerald Leads Through Winding Ways," *Sevannah Morning News*, April 15, 1934, Sec. 2, p. 10.

4. *The Letters of F. Scott Fitzgerald*, ed. Andrew Turnbull (New York, 1963), p. 510.

5. Cowley—TITN, p. xi.

6. This book is in the Clifton Waller Barrett Library at The University of Virginia. See "F. Highlights from the Barrett Library," *Fitzgerald Newsletter*, #11 (Fall 1960), 1-4.

7. "Introduction" to *The Great Gatsby* (New York, 1934), pp. viii, x.

8. Cowley—TITN, p. xi.

9. Peter Monro Jack, "The James Branch Cabell Period," *After the Genteel Tradition*, ed. Malcolm Cowley (New York, 1937), pp. 152-53.

10. Alfred Kazin, "Introduction," *F. Scott Fitzgerald: The Man and his Work* (New York and Cleveland, 1951), p. 17.

11. Cowley—TITN, p. xv. This view is shared by Wayne C. Booth, who states that the original version prevents the reader from identifying with Dick: "The achievement of the revision is, in short, to correct a fault of overdistancing, a fault that springs from a method appropriate to other works at other times but not to the tragedy Fitzgerald wanted to write. His true effect could be obtained only by repudiating much of what was being said by important critics of fiction about point of view and developing a clean, direct, old-fashioned presentation of his hero's initial pre-eminence and gradual decline." *The Rhetoric of Fiction* (Chicago, 1961), pp. 190-95.

12. Edwin S. Fussell, "Fitzgerald's Brave New World," *English Literary History*, XIX (Dec. 1952), pp. 291-306.

13. Otto Friedrich, "F. Scott Fitzgerald: Money, Money, Money," *American Scholar*, XXIX (Summer 1960), pp. 392-405.

14. Robert Stanton, " 'Daddy's Girl': Symbol and Theme in *Tender is the Night*," *Modern Fiction Studies*, IV (Summer 1958), pp. 136-42; D. S. Savage, "The Significance of F. Scott Fitzgerald," *Arizona Quarterly*, VIII (Autumn 1952), p. 206; Maxwell Geismar, "A Cycle of Fiction," *Literary History of the United States*, ed. Robert E. Spiller, *et al.*, revised edition (New York, 1953), p. 1299.

15. Leslie Fiedler, *Love and Death in the American Novel* (New York, 1960), pp. 301-2.

16. Albert J. Lubell, "The Fitzgerald Revival," *South Atlantic Quarterly*, LIV (Jan. 1955), pp. 103-4.

17. Fitzgerald Papers, The Princeton University Library.

18. Ford Madox Ford, *Joseph Conrad: A Personal Remembrance* (Boston, 1924), pp. 136-37. Fitzgerald's reason for using the "dying fall"—or the understated ending rather than the emotional one—is explained in a letter he wrote to John Peale Bishop on April 7, 1934: "I did not want to subject the reader to a series of nervous shocks because it was a novel that was inevitably close to whoever read it in my generation." See John Kuehl, "Scott Fitzgerald's Reading," *The Princeton University Library Chronicle*, XXII (Winter 1961), pp. 58-59—included in this collection.

Vance Bourjailly

Fitzgerald Attends My Fitzgerald Seminar

It is a frequent, not a favorite, fantasy of mine (Professor Short said) that one Tuesday afternoon when I arrive at Building UTBF to teach my graduate seminar in the work of F. Scott Fitzgerald, he is there—a pale, nominally handsome man, waiting for the class to start. He sits, I imagine, facing the desk where I will sit, as if he were to be one of the students, in the next-to-last of the five rows of seats in my small plain classroom.

Two of the dozen graduate students enrolled in the course are already there as well, a neatly dressed boy, a tall girl, who came together. We are all three (all four) a little early.

"Hello, Mr. Short," says the boy, whose name is Miles Hubbert, and the girl smiles blandly.

The intruder—well, the auditor. The auditor has placed himself as far away as is tactful from the student pair: not in the farthest seat left (left as I will face the class), but one chair in from that final, outside row. I have noticed that students in a small class-

Reprinted from *Esquire,* LXII (September 1964), 111, 113, 193-96, by permission of Russell & Volkening, Inc. Copyright © 1964 by Esquire, Inc. First published in *Esquire* magazine.

107

room always tend to group toward my right, and I wonder if he didn't realize this when he chose his place.

I knew who he was at a glance, of course, though my student pair, as well as those who will be along in a few minutes, may not. They are less accustomed than I to pondering those photographs; seeing him, I wonder again if the word "handsome" would have attached itself to this man had he not himself asserted that such was his appearance.

I am speaking, you understand, only of the appearance as pictured; I was sixteen when he died, and never actually saw him, nor is there any reason why I should have. But the man in the photographs has never seemed a handsome one to me. A masked man, rather, even in that young picture where he and Zelda and Scottie are all kicking out their feet in a dance step—the mask is debonair, merry, appealing, saved from smugness only in being somehow tentative, but only ordinarily good-looking. The bones which stretch the mask are grave bones, and their marrow is pain. Or is this the aftersight of anybody brought up on America's Monday morning? No matter. Surely one would rather look like, say, photographs of the young Hemingway. As one would rather look like Clark Gable than—could I cite these to my students? Hardly—Leslie Howard or Lew Ayres. (Not, no, that I look like any of these; in my photographs I think that I look bright-eyed and appalled, like a raccoon caught in the headlights of a car.)

As I turn from behind the desk my eyes meet his (not a raccoon's but a wild bird's); he seems to be asking me not to make known who he is. I could not refuse him anything, not today anyway, for he looks ill, incipiently middle-aged, drawn, painfully sober—but less out-of-place than you might think, sitting in a scratched-oak classroom seat with armrest for writing. Yes, he could be such a curious older visitor as we sometimes have—someone from another department of the University, an out-of-town guest of mine—to the students' incautious human eyes. They will register white shirt and quiet tie, but not the odd cut and wrong color of his business suit; it is the grey flannel which did not become unfashionable until I myself was in an Ivy League college, in the padded cut of the Late Depression. By it I know which period he is in—post-*Crack-Up*, Hollywood, *The Last Tycoon*, Budd Schulberg, Sheilah Graham, Arnold Gingrich. The last month. He is already, fatally forty-four. The final period.

Immediately I am confused at thinking of him in this way, confused because though it feels cold to me, I concede that he might like to contemplate the institutionalizing of himself that the division into periods connotes. In the twenty-three years since he died, this way of describing his life as if it were merely a career has become a convenience universally used by teachers and their students. There is not a youngster entering who could not (and as the most obvious kind of literary information) tell you the order of publication of his books, describe the critical and popular reaction to each one, and tell you how things were going for him when he wrote it. Yes, it would likely please him; it's a kind of attention which he died believing he would never get, nor even merit. Yet only six more years—all he'd have had to do was get past fifty, as Hemingway and Faulkner did, to see the processing start up: an emotional preface here, an M.A. thesis there, brief learned articles, larger ones, fictional treatments, studies at the doctoral level, whole books: an American becomes subject matter.

Four more students are seating themselves, Petey Luther among them; I wish this particular bright, harsh boy—my best student— had cut today. I hear his impatient voice arguing and it causes me such alarm that I suddenly consider dismissing the class. Fitzgerald and I could get a beer. Well, no, some coffee, I suppose. Yes, fine, Mr. Short. Just what he's come here for, the privilege of watching you drop saccharine tablets into bad coffee. And would you offer him a Hershey bar? The condemned man's last meal retasted (it was a Hershey bar, you know, that Sheilah Graham reports she gave him when he asked for something sweet, sitting there calmly in the Hollywood apartment, reading *The Princeton Alumni Weekly*, a few minutes before his heart quit).

(Almonds? That was a prep-school joke: male or female Hershey? I suppose he must have known that one. Ah, footnote writer, ah, diseased, ah, ghoulish, ah, Short, what a grand fellow and wise teacher the world has in you.)

"Will it disturb you if I attend today, Professor?" He asks it softly, placing his question under the clamor of youthful statement. His voice is cultivated, easy, touched with a protective whimsy to make it possible for me to say he must leave. From this I can guess that it is not my teaching of his work that he has come to hear, but what the young men will say. How could I not have known it?

"You'll be very welcome."

"But if you'd rather I left?" Painful courtesy, extending the anxiety of his moment, for it would destroy him were I to say, *Yes, go.*

"Please stay."

The students pay very little attention to this quiet conversation, for they are having a loud one of their own—a real, bickering, I-know-his-goddamn-batting-average-better-than-you kind of conversation about George Orwell's *Burmese Days.* Petey Luther thinks it's the finest novel of the twentieth century. Kevin Candlekirk, tricky debater, is leading the Luther kid on:

"Don't you think British Colonial matters are a little old hat? That's a topee, of course—Maugham's old pith helmet, Conrad's white cork."

"Yeah? Pith on you, Candlekirk," says Petey.

"Orwell was an officer, wasn't he, Petey?"

Such classroom manners, and with girls present, have startled my auditor, ending our own small discussion. Only the first boy, Miles Hubbert, has followed it, and he looks at the visitor rather closely. I have seen Hubbert on campus several times recently with this same tall, bland girl. (She is not his wife. She has a magnificent figure. She does not belong in my course. She is vapid.) Hubbert looks at me, and back at the pale man so seriously, with such open curiosity, that: no, even if he did do his undergraduate work at Princeton, I shall not let him guess. Hubbert, by the way, has three children, back in a Quonset hut across the river. Before the tall girl, whose name I can't yet remember (it is still early in the semester, the third class meeting, but now I do remember it: Betty Cass Collins), before that, Miles Hubbert used to be seen on campus with a cute, medium-tall girl called Janssy. I enjoy Janssy, who has taken a number of my courses, and would have expected her to be in this one. I feel that Hubbert is to blame for her not having registered for it. He must have changed extra-marital girls just about registration time. Since his contribution to a class session is to listen aloofly for two hours, not quite smiling, saying nothing, I resent him just a little. Two hours is a long time to keep things going, and an alert, pretty girl like Janssy is a great help. Hubbert's new girl (Betty *Cass* Collins; why *Cass* for Christ's sake?) is as quiet as he is; but not *like* he is; the quietness of cows is not like that of foxes.

"Who's asking you to repudiate Orwell?" Kevin Candlekirk cries, still teasing Petey Luther. "All I'm asking you to do, leaving Orwell out of it, is to name one first-rate novelist, just one, who was also a first-rate thinker? How about Dostoevsky, say, on politics? Or religion?"

"All right, he was a bum. Does that make Camus into a bum, too?"

"No, but it doesn't make *The Stranger* into *War and Peace,* either."

"What about Joyce?" Petey's tone isn't really angry, but if you didn't know him you might think it was.

"I don't think I'd want Joyce to marry my sister," Kevin says, and they all laugh, even Petey; but not Miles Hubbert, who only smiles slightly. And not the cow-girl, who cannot be presumed to have understood.

I glance at the auditor and see that the irreverence both pains and excites him. Joyce was a hero to him.

"We'll wait a minute or two," I announce. Petey and Kevin look at me, startled, I suppose, at the nervousness in my voice. "For the others," I explain. "The rest." My students are not prompt. Nevertheless, all are here, probably, who will be—eight out of the twelve—except for a girl named Eartha Hearn who is characteristically the least prompt and the most eager to be on time. Eartha has a paper due today and will wheeze in, distraught, apologetic, from a useless run through the parking area outside which I will wish she had spared herself. And here she is, hesitating at the door now, panting—smart, disheveled, overweight Eartha—and another girl behind her? Yes. Yes, by God, it is: Janssy!

"Professor Short," Janssy sings, gaily and all in a rush, pushing past Eartha Hearn and standing, legs open, on the balls of her feet, pink hand on the desk, leaning at me. "I registered late. Okay? I mean, I read *This Side of Flapdeedoodle* and Petey and Kevin told me what you said and they said, and the book for today, so I'm all caught up and I've even got a surprise, okay?"

I wince at Flapdeedoodle. I cannot see past her to know if he does. She blocks the view with soft sweater under open corduroy overcoat, and I can't speak. I have always liked to look at Janssy and whether she knows this or not, she does know that I'll agree to let her join the course. I nod, cannot speak, and try again to look past her at the pale man.

"But you have to sign my slip," she scolds and smiles and leans, all high coquetry, as a girl might demanding a kiss in public.

"After. After class, Janssy," I say, and she tilts her head, executes a ravishment, and slips into a seat by Kevin and Petey, ignoring the vacant one by Eartha Hearn with whom she came in. Nor does she look at Miles Hubbert, her former—what: lover, boyfriend, escort? Hubbert's face registers nothing more than its usual amused caginess.

"Let's settle down, please," I say, more crossly than I mean to. "We have a lot to cover." Kevin's hand goes up. "Yes, Kevin?"

"Something from last week," he says.

"All right."

"Just for perspective. We were talking about *This Side of Paradise* as if it were an undergraduate's novel," he says. "As if Fitzgerald were some kind of boy wonder. But look, he was twenty-three. Grad-student age, not a college kid. He'd been in the Army already. He'd even written one book and had it turned down."

"Yes," I say. "Of course. But you realize this was the same book, don't you? With a new title and some further revision. A good deal of it *had* been done while he was still at Princeton. As we were saying, portions of it had actually been printed several years earlier, in the *Nassau Lit.*"

"So much the worse, though, wouldn't you say? I mean, can you imagine a real boy genius like Rimbaud having the kind of ego where you're going to reuse everything you ever wrote, instead of the other kind of ego where you keep tearing it up, and striving for something perfect?"

"He didn't need Edmund Wilson," Petey Luther says. Apparently he and Kevin have been rehearsing this. "He needed a wastebasket."

I hardly dare look at the visitor, but I do. He seems—oh, quizzical, I suppose. Realizing that the young are never generous in making allowances for youth. Very well, then, I will be tactically cautious in opposing class opinion for the moment; I will wait for a better opening, later in the period.

Still, I must establish that concession is not to be my posture at any point today, so I say: "You know, a novel's a good deal harder to throw away than a poem. It's several years of work, not just a few days. And remember, the form itself, the novel, as an American expression shaped to the times, wasn't all laid out for him as it might be for one of you. It still had to be developed, it had to go through the hands of men like, well, like Fitzgerald himself as he was when he got done with *Gatsby*."

"Anyway, Petey," says Janssy, "different people mature at different ages."

"You were speaking of perspective," I say. "Perhaps it would be better to come back to this point later in the course."

"Rimbaud was probably a boring old man at twenty-three," the girl insists, and obviously this is for Miles Hubbert to hear. "Who'd want him?"

"Let's get to today's work," I say, but then I am reluctant to say what comes next. I know the visitor is going to be dismayed, but there is no way around it. I avoid looking at him and stare at bland, blonde Betty *Cass* Collins: there are two sorts of girls one looks at in class; the Janssy's, whom one enjoys looking at and forgets; and the Betty Casses, whom one sees with irritation, but whose coeducated bodies and sorority-group faces stay on in the mind. You feel you could do anything with such a girl, not because she seems sensual, but because she seems stupid. What bland blendings with blind blonde, bluntly—yes, Short. And sometimes you realize that an aura of such stupidity is something they wear to attract, like perfume, and means as little.

I continue to stare at Blah Cuss Cullings, and say what I have to say:

"Today, as you know, we will discuss the second book, the short-story collection, *Flappers and Philosophers*." But neither the clear-skinned, alphabetaface nor the unsuggestive knees of Miss Collins can hold my eyes away from his: they are stricken, the bird shot down. Why, on his only visit, must we talk about the least of his books? Why can we not be celebrating the great, achieved works, *Gatsby* and *Tender Is the Night*? Or discussing the tragic self-appraisal of *The Crack-Up*, in which everything is revealed but the one essential thing: how does genius survive the remorseless plots it makes against its own fulfillment? Hell, *The Last Tycoon* or even one of the other story collections. . . .

"Yes, Eartha?" It is odd about this bright girl, with her good mind and bad teeth, that she alone raises her hand when she wishes to speak, and will not begin until recognized. The rest, in my undisciplined class, push their way in and out of discussion at will. New York manners. Where were you brought up, in a subway?

"Yes, Eartha?" But Eartha Hearn is from New York, and is

polite; Janssy from a little town in Illinois, and steps on my feet whenever she feels it's her stop. Petey and Kevin are New York boys, true to type. Miles Hubbert? The East. I do not know where cow-girls come from, only that any time one goes away, another comes.

"Yes, Eartha?" There are others in the class, as indicated, but let them stay out of focus; they will get their C-pluses and B-minuses when the time comes. "Yes?"

Have I said, "Yes, Eartha," once or four times? Does the visitor sympathize with my uncertainty, or hold it in distaste? But I'm a scrapper, Scott, really I am, capable of rudeness too—no. No. Ten years of practice in academic manners and the false tolerance for other views which covers up uncertainty, to obtain unchallenged comfort for my family (the Professor's little daughters may play on even terms with doctor's children here), stand between this present and my scrapping days. I have became a fraud, who risks nothing but a hopeful good humor and a restraint which permits many impositions.

"Professor Short, about my seminar paper." Oh boy. Here we go. Eartha's excuse for not having done on time the paper that she's supposed to read here today. Some unanswerably drab female medical excuse, I suppose. And then what shall I do with two hours? Lecture? Without notes? Well, maybe—yes; yes, it could be best, at that. For me to lecture, spontaneously, out of the feeling I have, letting the words and ideas come as they will—this is something I haven't done since my instructor days when, some-times, I was so full of a subject (yes, in a sophomore lit survey course, even there, talking about *Tom Jones* or *The Scarlet Letter*!)—so full of it that notes would have been too confining, a hindrance. Hooray for menses, I will save the day.

"Professor, we made a change," Eartha says. "If it's all right?"

I frown, insincerely.

"I mean, Janssy wanted to share doing the paper with me. So I have a general paper on the book, and she'd like to talk about one particular story, afterward. I mean, since she's just joined the course? And. . . ."

Oh, all right. Let Janssy save the day, then. The girl's always been a bear for extra work. All right. I find a smile somewhere and present it. "Which story will it be, Janssy? *Bernice Bobs Her Hair?*" The best story in the book in many ways; the auditor has

a smile too. But Janssy shakes her head. *"The Cut-Glass Bowl?"*
A failure, but interesting for its ambition. Janssy smiles, and
shapes a "no" with her shiny lips. Three guesses, is that what
we're playing? Very well. *The Ice Palace* is a good story, and *Bene-
diction* very interesting indeed—which of these two?"

"*The Offshore Pirate*, Mr. Short," Janssy says.

"For heaven's sake, why?" There are worse stories in the book
—exactly two of them.

"I think I can show that it's important," Janssy says.

"Oh, come on Janssy," says Petey Luther.

(Do you know that story? About a flirt on a yacht, which is
boarded by a young man who represents himself as a rebel and
fugitive, bringing along his own jazz band? And woos, and finally
discloses that he's top-drawer eligible, just like her—oh hell. It's
preposterously bad.)

The auditor's face is with me, all the way, and yet resigned,
disturbed and resigned to whatever bumptions the young will in-
flict us with.

I nod to Eartha Hearn that she is to go ahead.

Her paper, which she reads carefully and not quite loudly
enough, is what I have come to expect from her: thoroughly re-
searched, critically conventional, a dull A. Yet last week I hoped:
so often, when one is finished talking over with a student what he
or she means to do in a paper, one does hope. The things they say
they want to write ("Perhaps try to get at what the flapper
personality really was, was it different from a flirt?") sound so
much more interesting than what they actually come back with
("Malcolm Cowley assures us that it was the flapper stories which
made Fitzgerald's reputation as a popular writer"). It takes Eartha
forty-five minutes to read this scintillating stuff, and I must pay
close attention to distinguish the words from the mumbles, so I
miss the detailed reactions of the auditor. I can sum them up,
though: beginning with intense interest, next twitchiness, then a
suppressed desire to interrupt and correct something (his hand
goes partway up), to a wandering of attention. By the time
Eartha's paper is done (". . . leads us to anticipate the recurrence
of these themes in later works"), he has actually, quietly, gently
gone to sleep.

Petey Luther's opening observation to Eartha wakes us up:

"You say there are two good stories in the book. I disagree."

"Hang on," says Kevin. "Petey disagrees."

"What is your disagreement?" I ask, straight-man Short, patsy of a bright grad-student's dreams.

"I don't think there are any good stories in the book. I like it even less than *This Side of Paradise*. Well, why? First of all, the book is full of race prejudice. I don't mean just the word nigger—I mean that Fitzgerald was so taken in by the South at this time that he was actually trying to be like a Southerner. Second point: there's an absolutely inverse relationship between how serious a story tries to be and how successful it is. When he gets serious, he's embarrassing; or obviously tricky; or sententious. When he's not serious, he may be slick, but he's still a snob, and a would-be-Southern one at that. Now. . . ."

"The man was desperately in love, for God's sake," Kevin says. I am shivering.

"May I finish, please, Kevin? Thank you, Kevin. Now it's true that two of the lighter stories come close to being good stories. And in fact each of them—*Bernice Bobs Her Hair* and *The Ice Palace*—has one beautiful line in it. Here's what I think is significant: each one of those lines is spoken by the chief female character, after a scene of catharsis. Right?"

I try to wrench myself out of my invisible trembling fit into the first character which occurs to me, and one I never play successfully, the sarcastic teacher: "And what two lines do you find up to your standards?"

The auditor's eyes are wild; the bird was shot down but only wounded, and now is crouching, hoping the dogs will pass his hiding place.

Petey Luther is opening his book.

"All right. One: in *The Ice Palace*. Sally Carrol has been driven back down South by the ice and snow and the ungracious Northerners. And this cracker, or whatever he is, comes driving up to take her swimming, and he asks her: 'What you doin'?' And she says: 'Eatin' green peach. 'Spect to die any minute.' Now that's a beautiful line, 'Eatin' green peach. 'Spect to die any minute.' All right? Now in *Bernice*, Marjorie's tricked her cousin into having all her hair cut off and ruined Bernice's appearance. So she sneaks in and cuts off Marjorie's hair—I mean, it's a real *Rape of the Lock*, isn't it?—while Marjorie's sleeping. Bernice is on her way out of town, anyway, and as she passes this boy's house, she throws

Marjorie's hair up on his porch. Listen to this: ' "Huh!" she giggled wildly. "Scalp the selfish thing." ' That's a beautiful line. Why? Why is it like the other one? Each of them expresses so perfectly, without Fitzgerald having to explain it, the return of self-assurance a little tease would feel after she's failed to measure up to a situation."

Miles Hubbert laughs out loud. Miles Hubbert!

"Let me answer him, Mr. Short," Kevin says, grinning excitedly. "May I?" This is not really politeness, but only a device for assuring himself the floor.

"Go ahead." I pin my wings on the slippery shoulders of Kevin Candlekirk. The visitor looks at him gratefully.

"I've heard Petey make many absurd statements," Kevin says. "But this one's got them all beat. He's asserting that somehow, out of context, a line—that is a moment—in fiction can be beautiful, more or less by itself. He discounts the author's preparation for it, as if aptness were a characteristic of the line regardless of its function in the story."

"You're willfully misunderstanding. . . ."

"May I finish, Petey? Thank you, Petey. I mean, it's like asking us to believe that 'Eatin' green peach. 'Spect to die' could go into the language, like a great epigram. Fitzgerald never wrote a great epigram in his life. In fact, every time he thinks he's got one, and he tries to slip in one of those polished, thought-out phrases, he ruins his tone—like look, how could anything but a really sharp story survive an opening line like the one in *The Ice Palace*?" He flips pages; I want to yell at him that this isn't necessary, but I can't. He reads. " 'The sunlight dripped over the house like golden paint over an art jar, and the freckling shadows here and there only intensified the rigor of the bath of light.' That's not part of the story, that's part of the notebook."

"You're not disagreeing with me, you're talking about something else," Petey says.

"But the lines you picked are wonderful because they're wonderful character lines. How could you have a wonderful character line in something that didn't have a wonderful character, and was therefore a pretty good story?"

"*I'll* speak about those stories," I suddenly hear myself cry out, above the opening cough of what would have been Petey's answer, and the room goes quiet. I am appalled. What was I going to do?

Claim that these stories are great works? I mutter: "After, after Janssy reads her paper on what story, what story? *The Offshore Pirate.*"

A boy might have a difficult moment trying to follow an outburst like mine—not a girl; a girl's sympathies are seldom general, and Janssy is quite ready, composed. Nerved up. She improvises a little preamble: "Petey calls Fitzgerald's flappers teases. I suggest there's no way of knowing whether that's true or not. We don't know what the word 'kiss' stands for in those stories. Anyway, what I want to show is that his understanding of immature relationships wasn't one-sided." She begins to read in a bold, take-charge voice, and the auditor's eyes are bright with hope: " 'If Fitzgerald exposes the heartlessness of shallow flirtation as practiced by his flappers, he also provides one of the most telling examples in literature of the male counterpart, the snow job. *The Offshore Pirate* is a story about a snow job so elaborate that even we are disappointed when we find out that the boy, who has been pretending to be a lower-class wild man abducting the rich girl, is nothing but a nice, safe rich boy after all. He was fascinating, sympathetic, worth our attention in the rebel character he assumed to snow the girl; he is unbelievably insipid, a perfect creep in fact, when we find out what he is really like, and no more than the flapper deserves. So well do they deserve each other. . . .' "

I could groan aloud. She is after Hubbert, of course, though it's the cow-girl who's blushing. By God, she really is rather embarrassed, and if only I could explain the situation somehow ("You see, Scott, this girl . . ."), he might be very interested. (There's no way. The students caught the teacher passing notes?)

" 'The girl in the story is not even a true flapper,' " Janssy reads on. " 'She's not like Marjorie or Sally Carrol or Bernice, who will at least put a little energy into their flirting. Ardita is passive, selfish. . . .' "

Whispering, now. Betty Cass Collins to Miles Hubbert. Hubbert back to Collins, nodding. Recovered, and with a dazzling smile for me in lieu of any spoken apology, Miss Collins simply stands, gathers her books, and walks easily out of the room and away. Mr. Hubbert? He's grinning now; I cannot say how comfortably, as Janssy, prim and grim and just a little shaken, reads on.

And, in fact, it is Hubbert's hand which goes lazily up the moment she is done reading. Should I ignore him, this first time he has deigned to speak? I look at the auditor, as if for permission, and see that he has understood and is fascinated.

"Yes, Mr. Hubbert?"

"Well, to borrow Petey's phrase, surely this is an example of willful misunderstanding," he says mildly. "The story is simply pleasant, isn't it? This is taking a joke seriously. That is, the peg's round, and I think the hole is pretty square. . . ."

"Hubbert!" I yell, furious. "What the hell makes you think you can speak offensively in my classroom?"

He looks at me, amazed. "I'm sorry, sir. What did I say?"

I look at the auditor—he, too, seems amazed. I look at Petey and Kevin and Eartha Hearn; they are all staring. Even Janssy is staring. Is it possible no obscenity was intended? It is too late to consider the possibility that Hubbert's was the first sensible comment in a twisted hour. I force my anger up a notch, spread its compass and rage on. "This has been the most extraordinary, stupid collection of misreadings, misinterpretations, snideness and bad criticism I ever heard," I shout. "How can you people be in graduate school and not have learned to read? Well? Do you think I'm asking rhetorically? I want answers—I may even want nine answers in writing. Well?"

Kevin's hand goes up. This time it's neither manners nor strategy, but sheer caution. He will get them out of having to write an extra paper if he can.

"Perhaps these stories mean something different to your generation than they do to ours, Professor Short," he says, his tone pure placation. He is offering me an out for unwise loss of temper, if I'll take it. The auditor (oh yes, I can tell) wants very much for me to take it; but I must refuse him now.

"Listen," I say, feeling triumph; for it is the exposed, the angry, injudicious teacher, railing at his students, who is giving them something of himself. "Listen, you're talking like a publisher. 'Generation' is not a critic's word, it's a word to sell books, and I hate it. Do you think I'm his age? Where's your grade-school arithmetic? I was born the year this book was published, and he was twenty-four. My father's his age, for God's sake.

"Listen, one winter in prep school, in the Thirties, long after his name had gone dim—when I was fourteen, and Sinclair Lewis was about the only writer that I'd ever heard of—I was caught smoking, and given a punishment. The punishment was called Five

O'Clock Study. It was for stupid kids who weren't passing, so they could have more time to get their work prepared. They had to work there, under supervision, in the school library. But I was never behind in any work. I was a disciplinary case. So the man in charge would let me read.

"When I'd finished all the Lewis, and whatever they had of Logan Pearsall Smith, I found Fitzgerald in the shelves, all green cloth and dusty. Three books were what they had: *Tales of the Jazz Age, Flappers and Philosophers* and *The Great Gatsby*. I read *Tales* first. God, how I remember sitting in that dim room, lost in a big leather chair, prevented from putting on my uniform to play shortstop for the school baseball team, which was my only athletic skill. I'd been looking forward to it all year—the sting of the ball when you go left and get the hard grounder, one hand, and the way your arm snaps when you throw hard. And there I was, off the grass, lost among the stupid and the slow, and I read a story called *The Jelly-Bean*. I was too frail and snotty a little shortstop to let myself cry, but I sat there staring across the library when I'd finished the story with a stare so sad that the man in charge came in alarm to ask me what was wrong.

"I don't know if *The Jelly-Bean* is a good or bad story. I only know that it still moves me to reread it—and it's Southern, Luther. It's Southern. And I know that if you can't keep yourself open to being moved that way by literature, then you are doing yourselves an unbearably grave disservice in committing your lives to the study and teaching of it. There's no critic worth reading or teacher worth hearing who's not a lover."

(I falter. There are things Petey loves, like Orwell. I shift my attack to clever Kevin. One does not speak successfully to a class, only to a student in it, letting the others overhear.)

"Let me tell you something foolish: as a boy, there in the prep-school library, I scorned reading *Gatsby*. The title, it seemed to me, implied that it would be about schoolboys—about a particular one with a grandiloquent nickname, as in the Lawrenceville stories, if you know them. We read that way, don't we, even titles, self-centering the world upon ourselves?

"So I passed it by and, by the time I knew my error, couldn't find a copy for seven years. Out of print. Unavailable. *Gatsby* out of print! It was on a troopship, going to Africa in 1943, that I did read *Gatsby*—borrowed it from the company clerk, read it once, straight through, missing a meal and a roll call or whatever the hell they called it, wouldn't get up and fall in, with the book

unfinished, and told the sergeant who came looking for me to
screw himself. Got myself on K.P. that way, and took the book
with me, and started through it again in the nauseous galley where
we washed trays and cups and slopped out food—and was the
only man on K.P. who didn't get seasick; I was too busy to get
seasick. Word by word, I read it, page by page, moved by everything: '. . . boats against the current, borne back ceaselessly into
the past.' Is that out of the notebook, Kevin? No, boy. That's out
of the tissue of his body.

"I was wounded. I suppose you all know that, and it doesn't
matter. I cannot tell you how bitter I was when I learned that the
way my leg was shattered, I would never be a whole man physi-
cally again; but I can tell you when it started not to matter. That
was when a friend brought a copy of *Tender Is the Night* to me
in the hospital in Italy. He was not even a particularly literary
friend, but he knew I'd been searching for that volume through
the bookstores of Casablanca and Algiers and Palermo and Naples
—for over a year, every time I got back to a city. It was an
Armed Forces edition, paper, with the cover torn off and Jonesy
told me that he'd traded a souvenir Luger for it, though he hadn't
cared for the book himself when he tried to read it. I won't try to
describe how it affected me then, but it was still affecting me two
years later, when I married my first wife, taking her for the image
of Nicole. I can't—I can't get away from that book: my second
wife, Mrs. Short, is more of a Rosemary. . . ."

I am starting to maunder. I catch myself up, and finish quickly,
not very pointedly:

"Shall we be biographers? There are two things in literary history which have made me swallow tears. Those are the letter
Dostoyevsky wrote when he lost his daughter, and the death of
Zelda Fitzgerald by fire. That happened late in the Forties, in a
Southern asylum. I was working for a newspaper then, hadn't
decided on graduate study, and you'd been dead—excuse me—
he'd been dead. Long years. The telegraph editor knew. Brought
the copy to my desk. . . ."

No. I am not teaching, nor even railing any longer. I am only
pleading, and have said nothing to them after all. But to him,
perhaps—I have always wished there was some way I could let
him know.

"Dismissed," I yell at the class. "Dismissed. Get out of here."

But my fantasy is not always that easy to end. There are various endings, to fit the different moods in which I let it play.

The abrupt one I have quoted is the one which satisfies me best.

In another, I look for him when I am finished speaking, but he has disappeared, evaporated in disappointment before he could hear me out.

Then there is one in which he goes off with Janssy, whom, of course, I love in a way which is remote only because it has to be. Thus, between them, he and she tear me in two.

But in the worst of my endings, he is still there, apparently waiting for me to get my books picked up, when Janssy comes to the desk to get her slip signed. While I am diverted, I can tell only that he has strolled across the room. And when she steps aside, thanking me, I realize that he is walking off, smiling, ignoring all the rest of us, friendly and at ease with Miles Hubbert.